TRUE MENTORS

ANSWERS TO THE QUESTIONS OF LIFE

GENE KATZ

TRUE MENTORS, LLC.
Highland Park, IL 60035

Printed in the United States of America
June 2004

--FIRST EDITION--

Library of congress cataloging-in-publication data is available

ISBN: 0-9755581-0-2

—FOREWORD—

As a society, we have grown careless in our ability to distinguish the true mentors, leaders and role models, from the undeserving celebrities. Money, fame and power should not alone be enough to make a person worthy of our respect and attention. The true mentors in society achieve great things while demonstrating values such as integrity, charity, responsibility, empathy, humility and purpose.
The true mentors in society do not seek publicity for their good works. The true mentors in society do their best to help others and make the world a better place.

—Dedication—

I dedicate this book to…

My loving wife, Tracy, who has given me so much in my life.
She is my sunshine, purpose and destiny.

My parents, Joseph and Inna, my brother, Matt, and my grandmother, Tamara, whose sacrifice and love made me who I am today.

God, whose presence has guided me throughout this project.

—Table of Contents—

—Chapter 1—

Introduction

Lying in bed at night, we have all been stricken by the inescapable grasp of the unknown. Who am I, and what do I want? Am I making the right choices? What does my future hold? Does my life have purpose? Am I happy? On these long nights, as we toss and turn, endless questions enter our minds, and it seems impossible to fit the pieces together. Family, love, work, society, God—no subject is left untouched.

Two years ago, before undertaking the writing of this book, I was a successful financial markets trader. I made a living by speculating in stocks and bonds, capitalizing on momentary inefficiencies in price. By my late twenties, as a result of a lucrative business, I had attained a lifestyle that I had never imagined possible. At times I made more money in one month than many people do in an entire year. I owned an expensive house, took frequent vacations around the world, and bought expensive jewelry for my beautiful wife. As a kid, growing up in a humble immigrant family, always aware of money problems, I had dreamed about how nice it would be to have lots of money and to be able to afford anything that I wanted. No more limitations, fears or insecurities. I had thought financial wealth must be synonymous with true happiness.

However, things did not work out as I had planned. Despite the wealth I had attained in the trading business, something was missing. I began to have trouble sleeping at night, as questions overwhelmed me. What was wrong? I was living the dream, and yet a void remained. I could not deny the overwhelming feeling that my life had no purpose. As a trader, I wasn't building anything tangible or having a meaningful impact on anyone's life. I certainly wasn't making the world a better place. In the world of trading, all that existed was buying and selling. The only thing that changed at the end of the day was my bank account, which kept getting larger. The dream of my childhood had come true, yet still I felt the need to make a change in my life. My success had not brought happiness.

In fact, I had grown cynical and disillusioned. Not only had my quest for money led me to question my own sense of purpose, but it had forced me to cross paths with some extremely unscrupulous people along the way. In the trading industry, I met a lot of people who lie, cheat, steal, and do just about everything they can for financial gain. After six years in the trading world, I realized that this was more the norm than a rarity. It was very disappointing to accept.

However, my observations were not limited to my profession. I soon came to understand that the disillusionment I had experienced in my industry was merely a symptom of much more extensive and universal problems. The corporate and political corruption, the constant over-emphasis on money, fame, and power, the deteriorating values and morals, the rejection of personal and social responsibility, and the absence of a greater purpose—these things could be found everywhere in our society.

Even worse yet, I realized that I had become part of the problem. I wasn't trying to help anyone or contribute anything positive to the world. Instead, I was simply striving for material reward. It felt so empty, but I did not know how to act on my feelings. What could I alone do to remedy these problems that seemed to have taken over our society? Instead of taking action, I grew cold, and learned to turn a blind eye to injustice and indecency. If it did not affect me directly, then it was not my concern. With the exception of my loving wife, and a few close friends, everything seemed meaningless. Innocence was lost, hope was gone, my faith had washed ashore on the rocks. After achieving great financial success and believing I had all the answers, I suddenly found myself in a place where nothing made much sense. Who was I? What did I want? What would be my fate?

Socrates once argued that "an unexamined life is not worth living." I believe he was right. Life is a constant growing-process. We need to comprehend the meaning of our lives in order to learn how to make the most of the time that we are given. Self-awareness, success, fulfillment, passion, faith and purpose, are they within our reach? If they are, then how do we achieve them, especially if we have strayed off course? And what about the other end of the spectrum—hopelessness, negativity, disdain, resentment, and indifference—how do we keep these powerful forces out of our lives?

I was stuck in a dilemma. How would I address these questions? Where would I search for the answers? Then, one sleepless night, I was struck with an epiphany. Throughout history, in times of conflict and confusion, people have always sought guidance from leaders, teachers, and prophets—wise men and women who have insight into the secret underpinnings of life. Suddenly it became so clear. In a society that suffered from having lost its sense of purpose, our ability to answer the questions that plagued us depended on finding the right people to lead the way.

With this insight in mind, I spent the next year seeking out these kinds of individuals, the "true mentors" as I call them in this book, and asking them questions about life. I traveled around the country in order to meet my subjects face-to-face, and discuss things like the principles of success, the secrets of happiness, and the meaning of life. I talked with Nobel Prize winners, world-renowned inventors and explorers, business visionaries, fearless leaders and great philanthropists. My goal was to gain insight into the personal qualities, inner feelings, and philosophies of these virtuoso masterminds, and to share those insights with the world.

This book is an account of what I discovered during my conversations with some of the most extraordinary individuals alive. The experience and knowledge that I acquired has changed my life. In the following pages, you too will have an opportunity to learn from the true mentors. With their help, we will uncover meaning, wisdom and understanding. We will ask them, and ultimately ourselves, many questions. Along the way, we may even find some of our own answers to the questions of existence.

—Chapter 2—

Independent Thinking

Steve Wozniak

Don't we all feel trapped by society from time to time? Family, colleagues, friends, everyone has their own set of expectations. There is a constant pressure to be someone, do something. Is it possible to live life by your own set of standards?

Steve "the Woz" Wozniak is one of the original founders of Apple Computer. Besides being a successful entrepreneur, he is accredited for being the inventor of the modern day personal computer. His accolades include the Presidential Medal of Technology and induction into the National Inventors Hall of Fame. Although he has amassed large amounts of money throughout his life as a result of his successful business ventures, Steve has given a large percentage of his money away to charity.

Today, Steve spends most of his time managing a small company in Los Gatos, California called Wheels of Zeus that is engaged in the research and development of new technology. He is a true techie at heart and enjoys playing with new toys. Among other things, the Woz enjoys video games, movies, fast cars and, more than anything, practical jokes. He has volunteered as a teacher in his local neighborhood school over the years, because he is fond of children and believes in the importance of education. Steve has three of his own children that he loves very much.

I met Steve at his Wheels of Zeus office in Los Gatos, California:

Q: In the early days of your career, would you have predicted that you would wind up developing a company like Apple Computer?

A: Absolutely not. I never thought that such things could happen. I never thought that I'd even have enough money to leave California for a trip. I just thought I was going to be a good engineer, live in an apartment and have a good life.

Q: But today, you are the person who is generally credited for putting together the first personal computer?

A: Yes, the first one that was good enough, that people would want. It really kicked off the computer revolution. It was the first time a million computers would be sold. It was personable; it was usable. It had nice things like color.

Q: When did you first get the idea for a personal computer?

A: It goes back to sixth grade when I got a transistor radio and my dad explained to me how at Lockheed they were designing new transistors. I said, "They're going to design better and better parts to make better transistor radios right?" He said, "No, they design them for the military, for NASA, and then what falls out is what people get." I always resented that. I always wanted to design stuff for normal people in their own homes. By the end of high school, I told my dad, "I'm going to own a computer some day."

Q: He probably didn't believe you, right?

A: No, he said it cost as much as a house.

Q: Growing up, did your father have the greatest influence on you?

A: By far. He was an engineer. Whenever I needed help, he taught me, but he didn't force me towards any direction. He also spoke to me about all of life's issues and values and how things work in the world. I remember our discussions; the words that came from him are exactly how I think to this day. I'm almost choked up thinking about it. He was just such a great man.

Q: That's where you started to develop your identity?

A: Yes. I also wasn't that social. That caused me to do a lot of internal thinking. I read (Thoreau's) *Walden* in ninth grade and that influenced me a lot.

Q: So you identified with being out in nature?

A: A little bit, but more the independent thought. Not being tangled up with a lot of the complexities of life. Today that's very much how I live. I try to keep things very simple, almost peaceful.

Q: Is it that why, over the years, you've given away fifty percent of your money?

A: Yes, virtually all of it. But I have enough to live on.

Q: Did you think that by giving it away, it was being applied toward a greater purpose?

A: Yes, I wanted to do it. It was too much to just have and hold onto.

Q: That's commendable.

A: I'd still be called wealthy, but my three ex-wives are much wealthier than I am. [Laughing]

Q: What would you tell other leaders and wealthy individuals in this world about philanthropy?

A: I don't go and tell other people what to do. It's a personal decision. Personally, I didn't want that extreme wealth, because I didn't feel comfortable with it. I never wanted it in my life.

Q: You have obviously not lived your life in pursuit of financial gain. How do you find fulfillment in your life? Do you have a personal philosophy?

A: Yes, just little philosophies of the world. I came up with a few. A couple of little guides that work for me, to make me happy forever.

Q: And what are they?

A: First of all, know inside that you're a good person. Knowing inside that you're good helps you to be happy. Second, don't set yourself up for unhappiness. Basically, just accept things as they are. This is how the world is. This is how nature is.

Q: Do you apply these philosophies to your personal and family life?

A: People are independent. The best thing you can do is to help your family members when they ask for help. Take care of them and talk to them. However, don't force them your way. Don't pick their religion, don't pick their colleges and don't tell them what they should study.

Q: Show them unconditional love?

A: Yes. And when they grow up they realize what they had, even if they don't at first.

Q: What has given you the greatest satisfaction in your life?

A: My head is stumbling through a bunch of pranks. [Laughing] They give me a lot of satisfaction. The fact that I can talk people into the most ridiculous things, and they believe it. No, I guess that's not it. I'd say having my first child.

Q: It changed your world?

A: I wouldn't say it changed my world. You used the word satisfaction. There was some kind of glee. Maybe even getting married at all; that was satisfying. That's probably it.

Q: Is that why you got married three times? [Laughing]

A: [Laughing] That's more just chance. I sort of found out that no matter what you want, you don't necessarily have a choice about getting divorced. Then I found out you can also make mistakes.

Q: Is there a secret to being married for a long time?

A: I would talk about that whole idea of finding a soul mate—somebody that's very much like yourself, and that you just talk to like any best friend. That's probably most important, but I'm just guessing.

Q: Do you have any regrets?

A: Yes, I wish I could have spent more time with my kids while they were growing up.

Q: Besides your family, what are the most essential things to you in your life?

A: Having fun. Smiles, smiles, more smiles than frowns, telling lots of jokes, playing pranks, having fun with your friends. Because when you die, you could be very successful with a lot of money, fancy houses, and other successful friends. Or you could just be one of these guys, like most of my friends who wander around doing interesting, unique things. They don't have much money, but they have laughs all the time. On the day that you die, how many times you laughed in your life is what matters.

Q: Humor seems like such an important part of your life. How come?

A: I don't know why, but when I was young, my mom said, "Have a sense of humor." I was always kind of a joke-player in schools. In recent decades, it has taken a turn into some of the most unusual pranks that anyone could ever pull off.

Q: When you're not busy playing pranks, are you one to follow your heart or your mind?

A: Heart. I also believe in following your mind, but so often what I end up telling everyone else in my life, my own children included, is to follow your heart.

Q: Are you a risk-taker?

A: I think it takes being a risk-taker to be successful. To have a huge success like Apple, you have to do something that other people aren't thinking about. If other people were able to calculate that it was going to make money, they would have just jumped on that boat and been there first.

Q: But how do you find that initial idea? What does it take to be a visionary?

A: A lot of believing in yourself and being independent. Not having to rely on other people's thoughts and ideas of what's spoken, said and read. In my mind, you must conceive an idea and just believe in what you believe in, even if the rest of the world doesn't see it that way.

Q: Is that why it is important to be a dreamer?

A: I think dreams are the most valuable things you take out of this life. It's just something close to your heart, because these dreams really come from you and not from other places. As far as making dreams real, that's what my life has been all about.

Q: You seem to have a lot of faith in yourself. What role has religion played in your life?

A: I consider myself a Christian, because I admire the man Jesus Christ based on some of the things that I've heard him do. But I don't belong to any particular religion, because I believe in being independent. I have my own personal sense of faith.

Q: From business to faith, you approach everything on your own terms. Where does your independent-thinking stem from? Have you always tried to not conform?

A: I was sort of an outsider during my school age, and I'm still not very social. I think a lot of my shyness comes from being afraid and fearful when I'm in social situations.

Q: What are you afraid of?

A: Probably, just not knowing what to do. Small talk, chatting, I never learned that.

Q: You never learned that, or you never really had an appreciation for it?

A: I can't tell which. I think it's because I didn't learn it, and then I deliberately would have a negative feeling about it.

Q: Is that why you left active management at Apple?

A: Actually I was always more inactive management. I was really an engineer. I don't like enemies; I like friends. That is how I was in life. I wouldn't run a company; I wouldn't manage. It's not something that I'm good at. I decided I would just be an engineer for life; that was my thing.

Q: You grew up in the nineteen sixties. Do you think society's values have changed during the course of your lifetime?

A: Oh yes, in the United States I think they have. There was a lot of this peace and love type talk back then; the key advice of the world was to be non-judgmental. I don't think that's how people are brought up anymore. Nowadays we've gone so far overboard on political correctness. We've lost most of our funny jokes; we had so much more humor then.

Q: Are there any aspects of our society that fill you with hope?

A: We have the freedom to dissent, disagree and to even criticize our own government. You can say horrible things about the president. That's your opinion; that's something you have the right to do. I'm glad we have this freedom, and I'm glad we have the protections of our legal system. I think our court system is very much the best.

Q: What are the biggest problems that you see in society?

A: Probably, the use of dishonesty to make it seem something is a certain way when it isn't.

Q: Does our society today have a defined purpose? Do we need a defined purpose?

A: A lot of us want a seven-second sound bite to give us the answer, because we don't want to spend a lot of time thinking about it.

Q: Is that attitude reinforced by the news media?

A: They write a story in advance, and they ask a bunch of phony questions of various people to fill-in answers. They will tell things in ways that are sometimes dishonest and untrue, and make it sound like it is the truth. It's a lot like how people work inside companies. They say one thing which kind of sounds pretty, but they're not really saying anything. They have good answers that hide the truth that people really want.

Q: Do you need to be skeptical? Is what you're saying?

A: Yes, don't put a lot of credit in what you hear. Also, I've learned that people are a lot more bigoted than they admit. Bigoted, meaning they want everyone to do things the way they do them. We always think that we're right about things more often than we are.

Q: How can society help people remain open-minded?

A: Education could get rid of a lot of society's problems.

Q: After everything is said and done, how would you want to be remembered?

A: As a good inventor. As someone who cared about his children's upbringing, and the future of the world being in their hands. Basically, we've made a lousy world in a lot of ways, a lot of problems. The younger generation can study what we did and maybe do better.

In many ways, Steve's independent thinking has led to his business success, because it has differentiated him from other people. Going against the grain and ignoring the status quo, he sees possibilities that others do not. This quality is a catalyst for his creativity, curiosity and invention. It allows him to be free of social norms and pressures, and thus enables him to take risk, follow his passion, and express his individuality.

More important than his financial success, is the fulfillment Steve's independent thinking brings him. He is comfortable in his own skin, and never feels pressure to be someone other than himself.

He realized a long time ago that life is about simplicity; conclude for yourself what makes you happy and then do your best to find it. Steve has found happiness from being an engineer, spending time with kids, and of course having fun. Jokes, pranks, laughs and lots of smiles—it's not a bad way to live.

So often we do things that make us unhappy in order to please society. So often we hide who we really are. There's no guarantee that independent thinking will lead to prodigious success as it did for Steve Wozniak. But even if you don't make as much money as your neighbor, does it really matter? When you take your own path in life, the destination will always be more rewarding, because it will always belong to you. Remember, no one knows more than you about what's right for your life. When you start to think for yourself and make your own decisions, you're less likely to have regrets. Never be afraid to follow your own path and deviate from the crowd. It's your life!

—Chapter 3—

Taking Action

Muriel Siebert

What good does it do to think independently, if you can't implement your ideas? Haven't we all felt that we've missed opportunities in our lives? Haven't we all doubted our ability to initiate and follow through on ideas? What does it take to be a person of action?

Muriel "Mickie" Siebert is best known for being the first woman in history to own a seat on the floor of the New York Stock Exchange. She later became the first woman to own a brokerage firm. Over the years, Mickie has built her firm, Muriel Siebert & Company, into one of the largest brokerage institutions on Wall Street.

Mickie has been a strong advocate for women's rights throughout her life. She feels that no one should have to undergo the discrimination and gender barriers that she once experienced. Recently, Mickie has become involved in a project with New York City schools, where she is attempting to teach inner-city kids the importance of a financial education.

To add to her achievements, Mickie has served as the New York State banking superintendent. Although she wasn't elected, she also campaigned to become a United States senator. Mickie has never been afraid to try new things. Her accomplishments in business, politics and philanthropy, have led to many honors including her induction into the National Women's Hall of Fame. Throughout her life, Mickie has done her best to make a difference.

I met Mickie at Muriel Siebert & Company headquarters in New York City:

Q: Can I ask you first, how you got your nickname Mickie?

A: There were three Muriel's in the school, all in my class. Two of us got the nickname Mickie, and one got the nickname Moo. [Laughing]

Q: What were your original intentions and goals when you came to New York?

A: Well, my father was a dentist, and he had a tough battle, which he lost, with cancer.

Q: How old were you?

A: Seventeen, eighteen…I was going to college and watching this. I was emotionally distraught. I was cutting class and playing bridge.

Q: So why did you eventually decide to drop out of college? Was it because you wanted to start working?

A: No, no, no, no, no.

Q: Was it your father passing away?

A: It was a major deal. For two and a half years there were operations. College didn't seem important compared to what I was going through.

Q: How did you get your first job?

A: I had been to New York once before, and I had been on a regular tour that included a trip to the balcony of the exchange. And I thought, gee this looks exciting. So I applied to Merrill Lynch. I went to the interview and they said, "College degree?" And I said, "No." As in no job. So I applied the next day, and they said, "College degree?" I said, "Yes."

Q: Did you feel a double standard, a sex barrier?

A: There were all kinds of sex barriers. On the other hand, I was doing very well. I was making great money.

Q: It seems like you never really paid attention to the sex barriers.

A: Oh no, I had my face shoved in. It was terrible!

Q: How are you able to overcome adversity like that?

A: You have to have a good sense of humor. You have to put your head down and say, "Get the little bastards."

Q: You have to look at the positive side?

A: Yes, I was doing well. Although every once in awhile I had something like that shoved down my throat, when I bought the seat, I was earning $300,000, $400,000; that was in 1967. That's not peanuts. I was earning more than doctors, lawyers and a lot of officers with the major companies. You really have to say "This is what I'm doing, who ever thought I could do that?"

Q: You were the only woman on the NYSE?

A: I was the only one for about ten years. For all practical purposes, I could say it was thirteen hundred and sixty-five men, and me.

Q: What would you say to people who encounter sex barriers to this day, or other forms of discrimination? How do you deal with that sort of thing?

A: Well, you have to analyze it and talk to yourself. And say, "Is this really the case or am I using it as an excuse?" If it's really the case, then you have to ask yourself, "Should I stay here or not. Do I want to subject myself to it or not? Can I handle it or not?"

Q: Sure, but how do you deal with it?

A: You have friends. You have interests. And you realize that the world changes. In my case, I realized I was helping to change it.

Q: What has kept you so motivated over the years?

A: At times, just seeing a challenge. I think the thing that motivates me now is the program I have going in the New York City schools. It teaches the kids about credit cards and checking accounts. There will be a class in every high school. There are two hundred and fifty high schools in the city.

Q: And it was your idea?

A: I brought the idea to the city, and then, in cooperation with the city, I structured the curriculum.

Q: What are some of the other social causes that you've been involved with?

A: I've been very active in the women's movement. It's very important to me that women are treated equally, and that they have equal opportunity. I was the third member of the Women's Forum, which was started twenty-five years ago. I've spent time and money helping it, and now it's international. I spend a lot of time on these things because I think they're important.

Q: Why are these things important to you?

A: Nobody should go through what I went through. It's just not necessary.

Q: I'm sure it helps women to have a role model like you.

A: It's an obligation when you're a role model. It's an obligation. At times, I wish I didn't have to carry it as much as I have carried it. But most of the time, it's thrilling, because you're influencing the lives of other people in a positive way.

Q: Do you think leaders have a greater responsibility to act in a certain way, by a higher standard?

A: Sure, you have to! At times, you do what you don't want to do, and you don't do what you'd like to do.

Q: What principles do you have to hold in order to be a good, effective leader?

A: You have to treat people the way you'd like to be treated. And you have to set the standard.

Q: You seem to see things before other people see them. What does it take to be a visionary?

A: Luck, and also having the time to think. You have to be able to concentrate on something. If you know your subject well, or if you can look at it impartially, ideas will pop.

Q: Has your attitude toward your work changed over the years?

A: Wall Street—I love it, but I don't love it. The business has changed. When I became the first woman member, I joined a group where your word was your bond, and you went broke before you broke your word. You don't have that today.

Q: Is everyone out for profit today?

A: In the last ten years, we saw a lot that shouldn't have happened.

Q: Do you think there is a general problem with integrity? What does integrity mean to you?

A: Honesty—treating people honestly. I studied Enron; I testified to the Senate last December. I called it "total moral bankruptcy." It was more than the officers of the company. It was the accountants. It was the lawyers that helped structure the deals and give the fairness opinion. It was the Wall Street banks. It was the Wall Street firms. It could not have been done without all five pieces.

Q: How would you advise other people to find the kind of work that they love?

A: Well, when you get stuck sometimes, you have to think about it. Be flexible and be honest with yourself.

Q: What were the qualities that helped you find your career?

A: Well, I guess I was born with a brain, and I found a field I could use it in. [Laughing]

Q: Has fate also played a role?

A: In some ways, a major part. I'd say fate gave me some opportunities, and I was sensitive and smart enough to recognize them.

Q: Is that something you've been very good at in your life, recognizing opportunities?

A: Everybody has the same opportunities, but not everybody sees it and says, "Hey, this is what I should be doing."

Q: We've talked about role models. Who were the people that made the greatest impression on you while you were growing up?

A: Well, my mother's brother, my uncle Frank had a lasting impression on me.

Q: In what way?

A: He was a businessman. He had a factory in Cleveland and another one in Arizona. They made plastic furniture covers, all of the covers for the floor models at Sears. I once said, "Uncle Frank, how do you do it?" He was so smart. He said, "You do your best, and you leave the rest to God." And that man had a peace of mind that was incredible. I thought about it many times. You do your best and leave the rest to God. He saw one doctor in sixty-five years…that's peace of mind. He was incredible.

Q: What kind of impact did your parents have on you?

A: My mother had a God-given voice. She was offered parts on the stage, but nice girls didn't do that sort of thing. She died with that regret and that frustration. When she got sick, her leg had to be amputated, and this put her in a wheelchair. She had to walk every hour with the walker, (to maintain) circulation in the other leg. But then she had another stroke the next year. They said, "Take your mother to the nursing home. She's a vegetable. She can only move the stump and one arm." I'd go to the New York hospital, and despite her condition, I'd get her to sing. Her voice filled the hall and they would say, "She has more mental capacity than we thought." I saw that frustration. It's terrible.

Q: Did she talk a lot?

A: She said, "Well, I can't act anymore, but I can still sing."

Q: Did seeing her bear that cross, influence you to avoid regrets in your own life?

A: Probably, probably. I have thought about that many times.

Q: Financially, how well-off was your family?

A: Not well-off; my father died basically broke.

Q: What kind of impact did that have on you, when you saw your father sick?

A: Money was running out. That probably gave me the drive to work hard. After my father died, my uncle took over supporting my mother. When I started to make money, I did.

Q: What does family mean to you today?

A: When you're single, your friends become your family. You make your own family. My friends are important to me.

Q: You have never been married. Do you have any regrets about that?

A: Not particularly. My friends are my family. And I know the influence I've had on people. I mean, it would be nice, but you know there are trade-offs. There are always trade-offs in every part of life.

Q: Do you think it's possible for a woman nowadays to have a really successful career and also balance a family life?

A: I know people who are doing it, but it's a job. And you have to meet a very good person that also wants the responsibility, the dual responsibility at home.

Q: What advice would you give a woman in terms of pursuing a business career?

A: They have to be realistic. And there could be trade-offs depending on whom you're married to, or if you're single.

Q: What are the most important things in life for you?

A: Well, altruistically I would say, using the knowledge and experience I have for the betterment of others. Along the way though, I'm somebody that has got a sense of humor and likes to laugh.

Q: How essential is self-awareness?

A: Very essential.

Q: Is it a constant growing process?

A: Growing, looking, reappraising. Who are you? Where are you?

Q: Faced with so many choices in life, how do you realize which path is right for you?

A: Part of it is instinct, being able to take a step without even knowing you're taking it. You can change direction without even knowing it. I'm not afraid to make mistakes. You're just not allowed to make the same mistake twice.

Q: How do you go from thinking about something, to implementing it?

A: When you get an idea, you have to be prepared to act if it's something important. You can't put it off. If you put it aside, you'll never get back to it.

Q: How crucial is it to keep hope and be an optimist?

A: It's crucial, but you also have to be a realist. Otherwise, you can keep making the same mistake.

Q: How would you advise other people to achieve happy, successful lives?

A: Life's a game, a serious game. [Laughing]

Q: So don't treat it too seriously on one hand?

A: And on the other hand, this is serious. It's your life. It's not a dress rehearsal.

Q: What role does faith play in your life?

A: Probably a significant role. I think it gives you a sense of decency. Knowing that there is some kind of a higher power. I believe there is. I think that tends to keep people in a pretty good balance.

Q: After everything is said and done, how do you want to be remembered?

A: She was nice, bright, and she did her share.

A poor young woman from Ohio moves to New York City all alone, and brings the mighty Wall Street community to its knees. When you meet her, she seems completely ordinary. Sure she's smart, funny and vivacious, but then many of us are. What makes Muriel Siebert extraordinary is her ability to act on her ideas, to implement and follow through. She does not get bogged down by distractions, insecurities, cynicism and adversity. She follows her uncle's advice, "Do your best, and leave the rest to God." What more can she do?

Mickie explains that you should always be prepared to take action. Never put off a good idea, because if you do, you will probably never get back to it. You must be ready to seize the opportunity. Once Mickie resolves to do something, she doesn't think about the reasons why she cannot; she just moves forward and does it. She may make some mistakes along the way, but she also has a lot of success.

We all make mistakes; that's a given. But it's a lot better in life to try and make mistakes than to regret never having tried. There's nothing worse than sulking over should of, would of and could of been. It's important to be smart and practical, but that doesn't mean that you shouldn't be a person of action. Choosing to take action is not a natural talent, it's a decision. It's about resolving to do something, and then seeing it through to completion. Whether we realize it or not, we all have this ability.

—Chapter 4—

Risk-Taking Ability

Bernard Marcus

How do you decide whether a risk is worth taking? Do you have to take risks in order to become successful? Is it natural to be afraid of risk?

Bernard "Bernie" Marcus is the founder of Home Depot, and the company's original chairman and CEO. It was his vision that created the company in 1979. Before building Home Depot, Bernie had a long, distinguished career in the retail business. During his career, he managed large national chains such as Two Guys and Handy Dan.

When Bernie started Home Depot, he was in his fifties, and financially broke. Although his former business ventures were extremely successful, almost everything had been taken away from him due to unscrupulous business associates. He put all he had left into his new business venture, and even moved his family half way across the country to Atlanta, Georgia. Through relentless work ethic, Bernie and his partners made Home Depot the company it is today.

Much of Bernie's motivation has stemmed from wanting to provide for his family—his parents, his wife and his three children. He grew up very poor, and always felt the pressure to make his own way in life. His Jewish heritage also has played a large role in defining his life and value system. He often talks about various Jewish teachings, especially those relating to community service and work ethic. As a child, the horror of the Holocaust also had a large impact on him.

Bernie is one of the most prominent philanthropists in the world. He has established the Marcus Foundation, which he now actively runs on a full-time basis. Through this organization, Bernie and his wife Billi contribute to a wide array of causes including children, free enterprise, religion and medical treatment. This billionaire has pledged to give away much of his vast fortune before he dies.

I met Bernie at Home Depot corporate headquarters in Atlanta, Georgia:

Q: What does it take to overcome adversity?

A: Well, I think that it helps to know that if you fail, you're dead. We had no money, none of us had any money. And this was a shot. And if we didn't succeed, all of us were finished. I'm talking about finished.

Q: You just put in everything you had?

A: Yes, we moved our families. We separated ourselves from our support groups. We came to Atlanta; we knew nobody here.

Q: So it was a risk?

A: We believed in the strategy. It's not as though we did it in a vacuum. We knew what customers wanted. They wanted to be able to buy whatever they needed in one place. You can't sell people what they don't want. Prior to a Home Depot, in order to recondition a house or build a house, you'd have to go to a plumbing supplier, a lighting supplier, a lumberyard, a building material store and a paint store.

Q: How were you able to know that before anyone else did?

A: My retail experience has never been on the twenty-first floor of a building. My retail experience has always been in the stores, on the floor, talking to customers, talking to vendors, talking to suppliers and talking to employees—that's a retailer. You show me a retailer that spends all of his time at the corporate headquarters, and I'll show you a business about to fail.

Q: But how are you able to take that kind of risk and put everything on the line?

A: We believed in it!

Q: You had confidence in yourselves?

A: Yes, we had confidence that it was right, but I must tell you the first year was pretty bleak. It was scary, and we were slowly but surely eroding all the finances.

Q: How did you make it through that?

A: Well, when you know your life is on the line, and you know that your career is on the line, and you're the breadwinner of your family, then you make it work.

Q: What does it take to be a successful entrepreneur?

A: I think that entrepreneurs are risk-takers. An entrepreneur has to be a little crazy to start with. And I think that this group of people fit the bill. I think that we were certifiably insane. [Laughing] You have to believe passionately in what you're doing. If you can't convince yourself passionately that this is the right thing, you can't convince other people. You have to be able to knock down doors. And you have to be able to deal with failure. People that can't deal with failure, can never make it as an entrepreneur. You just can't do it. I can't tell you how many times during that first year or every year thereafter that there was a blow, there was a blockade, there was some kind of difficult situation that would depress most normal, ordinary people to the point where they would throw in the towel and give up. We didn't let that happen to us. We found a way around it.

Q: How do you achieve that kind of persistence?

A: In my case, the fact that I was fired from my job before starting Home Depot has always stayed with me. Therefore, you never become self-assured. You never become smug about what you're doing. To this day, I always feel like something is crawling down my back. I'm always running knowing that if you're the fastest guy out there, the crowd is always right behind you.

Q: Did you want to show those people that fired you, look what I've done?

A: Yes, we did obviously. They went out of business by the way. But that was not the overwhelming desire. For me, my real motivation was success and being able to take care of my family. I mean that was the overriding thing. I came out of a poor family. No financial support. If I failed, I didn't have a rich father…the word was failed. I mean it was like dead. I was finished.

Q: Growing up, your parents were Russian immigrants, and you came from a very modest financial background. What kind of effect did that have on you?

A: There are certain things that are instilled in you at an early age. I mean, when money is tight and food is scarce, bills don't get paid.

So there's a certain amount of insecurity that you have.

Q: Did it make you work harder you think?

A: Listen, I worked from the time I was thirteen, and I didn't resent it. I did it because that's what you did. That was normal. All of my friends had the same problem. We were all poor where I came from.

Q: Did you have any role models growing up?

A: My mother was a role model. She was a wonderful woman, a great philosopher. She could get along with anybody. She had this great belief that you could do anything in America; that this was a great country and you could be whoever you wanted to be. All you had to do was work hard, put your nose down and stay with it. Don't lose faith in what you are and who you are. And she was right.

Q: What role has education played in your life? You went to Rutgers.

A: Not much. I was running a business at the same time. So I basically worked during my college education to pay for it.

Q: You got your worldly education from work?

A: I got it from work.

Q: What do you think has motivated you throughout your life, at your core?

A: A desire to become successful. And what does success mean? Success means to be able to take care of your family. To be able to provide for all of those that you want to take care of. Success, because of the Jewish life that I grew up in, was *Tzedakah*, which means to give back to the community and to help those who are not as fortunate as myself.

Q: So you've felt a social responsibility from your early years?

A: Always, always. I have been working with charities for most of my life.

Q: Even before you made a lot of money?

A: Sure, sure. I did a lot of those things, because I felt a social consciousness about these issues.

Q: Where does that come from?

A: It stems from my mother. It stems from her upbringing. She used to say, the more you give, the more you get. When we resented her giving away our candy money or our ice cream money, she would say, "It will come back to us…you'll get more." So I grew up believing that concept, and it became part of my fabric.

Q: It was part of your fiber?

A: It was part of our fiber. People come into our store and they would have no money. A woman I remember came into one of our stores with five dollars. This little old woman, she was in her eighties and she had five dollars. And she went to the lumber department, said she had a leak in the roof and the water was coming in. And what could the five dollars do for her. Well, the young man that she talked to got so emotional about it, he took it to the manager. And the manager said, there's nothing, but let's go take a look at the roof. He went out and looked at her house and saw the roof was gone. I mean there was no roof. So a week later, he had twenty or so associates out there on their own time, and he came to us and asked us if we would supply the materials, which we did. And it became a training session on how to put a roof up. Today, we do that at every single store in the company.

Q: I wish more companies did that.

A: Well, today, a lot of companies are doing that. But they do it for publicity. We did it because it was the right thing to do.

Q: What has your family meant to you in your life?

A: Well, what do you expect me to say? [Laughing] My wife has been the greatest supporter that a man can have. In fact, retail is a lousy business. Retail is not a nine-to-five job. Retail makes a family very, very difficult, because you're there all the time. I'm talking about fifteen, sixteen-hour days, six or seven days a week. So the sacrifice of the family is enormous. And she has been just the greatest supporter that a man can ever have. I've been married thirty years.

Q: Is it possible to balance family with being a successful businessman?

A: There are people who are able to do it. I guess it depends on the business. I guess that if my kids wanted to do it today, there's the financial backing. They wouldn't worry about it. Remember, I didn't have the financial backing. It wasn't the case that I didn't want to do it. No, I wanted to be there for the kid's baseball games. Could I do it? No, I couldn't do it until we were successful. So the balancing of life, I'd like to say that you can do it, but I can tell you that I don't know many people that do that well.

Q: There's always give and take?

A: It's always give and take.

Q: Would you say you felt a pressure to achieve really tremendous things, great things in your life?

A: I always thought about just being as good as I possibly could be. And that would be satisfactory to me. In this case, it ended up being pretty outstanding.

Q: On a more philosophical note, what do you believe is the meaning of life?

A: I think being able to get satisfaction out of your life and live comfortably. And have a moderately happy life. [Laughing] I mean we all have challenges. We all have disappointments. But despite these disappointments, it's so important to have the ability to enjoy the good things in life. You know, sometimes just a sunset is a beautiful sight and you have to be able to appreciate that sunset. A lot of people can't do that. A lot of people are so negative; they are so full of anxiety and compulsions, that the simplest things don't give them enjoyment. I think that simple things give me enjoyment. I like walking, I like looking at things and I like listening to people. There are a lot of things out of life that I enjoy.

Q: But you need to know what you want out of life and where you want to go?

A: Every year I used to set a goal for myself. I would have a discussion with myself and say where do I want to be next year at this time? If you don't have a goal, you don't have any place to go.

Q: What happens if you work your hardest, and still fail to achieve your goals?

A: You need to have interim goals that are achievable. It's very easy to disappoint yourself, and you can disappoint yourself if you set goals that are not achievable. The goals have to be realistic, but they also have to be stretch goals.

Q: Stretch goals?

A: Yes, I mean nothing can be a slam dunk. Why would I wake up in the morning if I've already achieved my goal?

Q: You have to challenge yourself?

A: You need to have a challenge, and that's what I call a stretch goal.

Q: Are you one to follow your heart or your mind?

A: Always follow your heart and your mind! It's a combination, absolutely without question. I'm very passionate about whatever I do.

Q: How do you go from thinking about something, to doing it? How do you prevent getting stuck and not being able to execute?

A: You have to be realistic about what your abilities are. Most people get stuck because they think that they can do everything, and nobody can do everything.

Q: You have to learn to focus?

A: You have to get the most out of your abilities. The truth is that if you're not an entrepreneur, you can't make yourself an entrepreneur. If you're not a genius, you can't make yourself a genius. We have a tendency to set goals for ourselves that are not achievable because we don't have the real stuff to do it. Then we get frustrated, and in many cases, we begin to blame other people. You can blame everyone else, that's easy. But to say, "I didn't get there because I'm a dumb imbecile." That takes character.

Q: Or because you'rc lazy?

A: Well, all of those things. Because you're lazy. Listen, I've had conversations with people here that were coming to me, ready to chew my head off. One person said, "I should have been the head of that department." And I said, "You know why you didn't get it? Because of you. No one likes you. You don't have the ability to deal with people. You're a terrible leader. You don't listen to anybody. Why are you blaming everybody else? It's you. Straighten out your act." I'm happy to say that I changed a lot of people's lives by getting them to think in those terms. So what I'm saying is, when you set a goal, it has got to be realistically within your reach, with your abilities, your acumen, your background. That's why you have to achieve everything in increments.

Q: How important is it to keep hope and be an optimist?

A: Oh, very important. I'm a born optimist. Failure mostly is in your mind. If you think you're a failure, you are a failure.

Q: Do you feel like you made your own destiny?

A: I think that there's no question about it. I think that my optimism, the fact that you could never knock me down, took me far in life. When I get knocked down I'll get depressed. It could be an hour, it could be five hours, it could be a day, but the next day I wake up and I'm ready to go again. There's the other issue of taking responsibility for your own life. Most people blame everybody else for their failures. I'm telling you that you got to accept responsibility for what you do. You got to stop covering up. We waste so much time covering up the mistakes that we made.

Q: What's the value of making mistakes?

A: It's a learning experience only. You don't second-guess yourself. You say why did I do it? What came out of it? How dumb was it? And then it becomes a lesson not to do anything like that again. It's only meant to help you in the future.

Q: What's the value of being a dreamer in life?

A: Dreamers create the future.

Q: Are you a dreamer?

A: I think so. I love dreamers and I try to surround myself with dreamers. But I'm very careful to surround myself with practical people also. You need to have somebody that executes. It's very important.

Q: What does integrity mean to you?

A: It's part and parcel. I watched the Enrons of the world; I can't even fathom it.

Q: What do you tell young people who see that in society there are very successful people who have no scruples?

A: If you can't live with yourself at the end of the day, what's it all worth? A dollar made dishonestly, is not a dollar made. How can you live with yourself?

Q: Is it about redefining success?

A: Maybe for some of these kids who come out of Harvard Business School, where they were never taught ethics. In the world that I grew up in, most of us never behaved that way. We would never think of lying and cheating.

Q: Does society overemphasize money in its definition of success?

A: I don't think that money is dishonest. I think that success, making money, there's nothing wrong with that. That's the free enterprise system. I'm very, very proud of the fact that I'm very wealthy.

Q: Making it in a dishonest way, that's the problem.

A: Making it dishonestly, those people should be locked up and set apart from society. They don't belong in society.

Q: How much of a role does fate play and how much do you have control over?

A: Everybody is afforded an opportunity at some point in life. Most people never take the risk and life passes them by. And you hear the sour grapes of how unlucky they were. I'm sure there are many people that say how lucky I am. They don't know the pain and suffering that I went through to get where I am. They don't know the disappointments. It's not luck! These are all things that could have happened to other people. I took shots.

Q: You kept putting yourself in the right positions?

A: And I always put myself in a position of danger also. You show me a guy who's lucky. I'll show you a guy who's successful. I'll show you a guy who's smarter than the next guy.

Q: You've got to make it happen. Nothing falls in your lap.

A: Never does. Look at Bill Gates. Bill Gates's success is based on somebody else's stupidity. IBM turned him down. If IBM hadn't turned him down, Bill Gates would not be who he is today.

Q: What role has faith played in your life?

A: Very important. It's part of the ethics that drive you. You can do anything, if you have faith in yourself and other people.

Q: Does it give you a sense of greater purpose?

A: It gives you a better sense of yourself. You can't blow these things out of context. I don't sit back here and tell you that my whole life has changed because of some great picture in the sky that I had. It's not true. Remember, it was survival.

Q: Did you have faith in a greater meaning that you were here to do something more?

A: No, (but) there may be people that feel that way. I was very practical and I just wanted to feed my family. So I had to be smarter than the next guy. I had to do what I thought was the right thing to do.

Q: So what's the secret to being happy and fulfilled in your life?

A: Let me give you my profound theory. My profound theory is that there are people who are successful financially, who are miserable human beings. When you spend time with them, you want to kill yourself (because) they're depressive human beings.

It's feeling good about yourself and feeling good about what you've accomplished. It's enjoying life and not letting the world put you down. It's not letting circumstance put you down. It's being satisfied with who you are. You don't have to be as wealthy and successful as the other guy. You could be a guy who earns a living, works forty hours a week and gets a lot of happiness out of his family, his house and playing ball with his kids. It's about being satisfied with what you've accomplished and also understanding who you are. You can't be who you're not.

Q: How about society as a whole? What do you think the future holds?

A: I think the houses of worship will play a very important role in defining who kids are today, at least those religions that teach ethics. There are many religions that teach only hatred, but I'm talking about the religions that teach ethics. They are very important for children today. I think they need that. I really think they need that backing.

Q: After everything is said and done, how do you want to be remembered?

A: We only live for one moment. Our lives, in the context of civilization and time, are a blip on the screen. And I'd like to know that I was remembered for all the good things that I did. It's what you leave behind that's important. That people don't forget you easily and remember the good things you did. You hope that the good things far outweigh the bad things.

What most astounded me about Bernard Marcus was his tolerance for risk. He believes that successful people need to be risk-takers. How many individuals would risk starting a business when they're fifty years old, financially broke, and responsible for supporting their family? In theory, what happened to Bernie could happen to anyone. On some level, every single one of us has such an opportunity at some point in our life. However, nothing just falls in your lap. You have to make it happen. You have to be willing to take a risk.

So many of us are reluctant to take risks, because we are afraid of making mistakes, looking stupid or being considered a failure. Even calculated risks can seem very frightening. It's difficult putting yourself on the line, trying something new and unknown. However, what most of us don't realize is that there's no reason to be scared of risk; most of life is a risk. We like to think that everything is under our control, but ultimately, what we become, who we marry, where we live, whether we succeed or find happiness, and even how long we live—everything is uncertain.

Once we accept that risk is a part of our everyday lives, it's no longer that difficult to assume new risks. For instance, in business, many of us are scared to start our own enterprise. Working for someone else seems much more stable. However, what guarantee do you have that you won't get fired for reasons beyond your control? It's always a risk. Bernie Marcus achieved what he wanted, because he was willing to go after it. Family, love, passion, success—what do you want in your life? Take a risk and go for it!

—CHAPTER 5—

INTUITION

VERNON SMITH, PH.D.

Even if we're able to take action and assume risks in our lives, how do we know what decisions to make? Do we have an inner-voice that tells us what we should be doing? Can we trust our intuition?

Vernon Smith, the Nobel Prize winning economist for 2002, is regarded as the father of experimental economics. His constant breakthroughs and insights have resulted in over 200 hundred papers and books that have helped push experimental economics to the forefront of economic theory. Through laboratory experimental methods, he has empirically provided evidence for a range of economic models. Vernon's work has created a bridge between textbook theorization and pragmatic application. Unlike most academics, many of his experiments are designed to find solutions for real world problems. An intense believer in interdisciplinary study, Vernon contends that many of the answers to economic questions can be found by analyzing other, related subject matters, such as political science, history, biology, anthropology, archeology, sociology and psychology.

Vernon received his Ph.D. in Economics from Harvard University. Throughout his career, he has been a professor of economics at various educational institutions including Brown University, California Institute of Technology, and most recently at George Mason University. Vernon is married to Candace Smith, a dedicated, award-winning teacher, and together they have several children from each of their former marriages. Vernon and Candace enjoy each other's company, and, among other things, love to travel together.

Physically, Vernon looks nothing like a Nobel Prize winning economist. He more resembles a motorcyclist. His most striking feature is his graying blond hair, which hangs down to the middle of his back in a long ponytail. His garb is also quite eccentric. On the day that we met, every one of his fingers displayed ornamental silver rings of Native American origin. From his groundbreaking economic theories to his radical sense of style, it's apparent that Vernon marches to the beat of his own drum.

I met Vernon at his office in the economics department of George Mason University in Arlington, Virginia:

Q: In the early days of your research did you conceive of the impact that your work would have on the field?

A: No, I didn't have the remotest idea. I don't ever think in those terms. I was doing it because I found it very exciting.

Q: What would you say were the original intentions of your research?

A: Curiosity. I was trying to relate abstract economics to experience.

Q: Where did your curiosity actually come from?

A: (It's) hard to know. I think part of it is a curiosity about how things work; a curiosity about the hidden meaning in things. It takes you a long time to realize that things are not necessarily as they look.

Q: Has finding the work that you love been the secret to your happiness?

A: Yes, but I think in some ways, I'm a pretty happy person anyways. I'm basically an optimist. I have a tendency to look at the best side of things.

Q: How did you decide on a career? Is it serendipity or must you really search for it?

A: Oh, both. I think when a good opportunity pops up, you have to exploit it.

Q: You have to stay open-minded and flexible, so that you can see that opportunity?

A: That's a good way to put it. You sort of hang loose. I think one of the things I learned to do is look for more than what I expected. It's very important to think outside of the box.

Q: You've certainly done that within economics. It seems that what's most interesting about your work is how you combine so many different fields of study in your research.

A: Yes, that is a natural extension of trying to understand the world. People are going through the same song and dance in every field; they just don't see the connection.

Q: Do you teach your students to be interested in many different subjects?

A: I always tell students to not read too much in economics. Read widely outside of economics. In economics, it's always the same kind of models being used over and over again. You're more likely to get some fresh inspiration from some other field. Read nature, science, meteorology, astronomy, physics, biology, archeology and anthropology.

Q: So how about philosophy? What do you believe is the meaning of life?

A: I think that everybody has to find their own meaning. I found my meaning in what I've done and the way I've lived.

Q: What are the most important things for you in your life?

A: Well, I think the recognition and respect for my actions. My actions really define who I am. I hope my actions are perceived as doing more good than harm.

Q: Faced with so many choices in life, how do you realize which path to take?

A: I always seem to know what to do, and I can't even exactly tell you why. I don't deliberate on things like that. It's always a question of what am I satisfied with and what interests me.

Q: Your future appears in front of you, and you go with it?

A: Well, the next step appears in front of me, and it eventually becomes the future. [Laughing] The future is a series of small steps in which I'm not particularly thinking about the long-term plan.

Q: You follow your present interests?

A: Yes.

Q: Are you one to follow your heart or your mind?

A: I guess if you're thinking about the conscious calculating mind versus the intuitive heart, then I follow my heart.

Q: You're very in tune with your intuition?

A: Yes.

Q: Say you have this great idea, how do you execute it?

A: You first have to satisfy yourself that your hunch is really a good idea and not just some fantasy or thought that has no merit. You first have to convince yourself that there's something there.

Q: And then I guess at some point you need to have resolve and say I'm going to do this?

A: Yes, yes. And you can get negative feedback in the beginning, but don't abandon the idea. The first impression of others shouldn't tell you what to do.

Q: You've got to have confidence in yourself?

A: Yes, if you don't have confidence in yourself, then you'll throw away a good idea just because someone laughed at it. People, when I first started, couldn't understand why I was doing experiments.

Q: I'm sure it takes quite a degree of optimism to be a revolutionary thinker when everybody is telling you that you're wrong?

A: Yes, you have to challenge them. [Laughing]

Q: Is there room to be a dreamer in your life?

A: Oh yes! Dreams are the substance of accomplishment. In fantasy all things are possible!

Q: And that applies to science also?

A: Yes, yes exactly!

Q: Do you believe that who we are and what we want out of our lives changes over the years?

A: I think what we do is learn more about ourselves and in that process you probably do change, no doubt about it. I have certainly changed in various ways. But there's also a sense in which I'm not any different than I was when I was seven years old. I don't feel any different. I think more than anything it's learning the implications of who you are.

Q: How essential is it to be able to overcome adversity?

A: Well, adversity is there to be overcome. You don't want to be taken by it. You have to believe in yourself. That carries you passed adversity.

Q: How would you advise other people to become successful in their lives and achieve great things?

A: I can't. Because too much of what I have done has not been driven by some kind of calculation or plan.

Q: So would you say choose your own path?

A: Choose your own path. Do what you like to do. Don't worry. What else do you need? If you like what you're doing and you get satisfaction from it, that's good enough.

Q: What's the secret to being happy and fulfilled in life?

A: You don't get anywhere by bitching. It's not where you begin, but it's where you end up. You know, the cab driver on the way to the Reagan Airport yesterday, he told me that he has worked as a cab driver for thirty years. I asked, "Why do you do that for thirty years?" He says, "Because I like it, I can choose my own hours of work, I'm free." And he says, "I might not earn as much as a result, but if I did anything else, I wouldn't be happy." He's perfectly happy! He says, "The other thing I learned is don't look up, look down. If you look up, you will see the people who have more than you. If you look down, you will see the people who have less than you. It will make you appreciate your life."

Q: It makes you feel fortunate about what you have.

A: Yes. The only thing that I would add to that is you also look back and see how much better off you are than your parents, grandparents and the ones before that. So the rule is to look back and to look down. [Laughing]

Q: I think that's something we all need.

A: The cab driver is Pakistani and I told him, "I'm sure this is in the Koran too. Thou shall not covet thy neighbor's possessions." He said, "Oh yeah, we have that." [Laughing]

Q: Do you believe that our society places too much emphasis on money?

A: [Laughing] No, because you don't have to join it.

Q: Do you think our society needs a more defined, clearer purpose?

A: Well, I don't know. Who would define it? It's defined by the sum total of us. I think that the old values, family and religion, are as important as ever. I don't see some kind of discontinuous change.

Q: What has given you the greatest satisfaction in your life?

A: My work. The most satisfying part about it is its quest for the understanding and comprehension of things.

Q: Is there anything else outside of work that you would want to be remembered for?

A: I hope my family will appreciate me as a person rather than a person who generates papers and Nobel prizes.

Vernon talks a lot about the importance of trusting your intuition. The right course of action seems to just present itself to Vernon, but that's because he is always open to new ideas and opportunities in his life. Once he absorbs all the information, he goes with what he feels in his gut, and has faith that his hunches will lead him in the right direction.

Each one of us has an inner voice that knows many of the answers. It usually tells us what is right and wrong, what we want in our lives and even who we are. As a result, often times the answers become infinitely clear. However, for whatever reason, many of us still choose to ignore this voice. We analyze and rationalize to the point where the right course of action no longer seems reasonable.

When you follow your gut feeling and make a mistake, it is usually a learning experience. At least there is no regret about passing up something that you really love. Most of our bad choices in life occur because we ignore our instincts. Instead, we look at what other people are saying or doing, and sheepishly follow. When you're doing what you really want in your life, what else do you need? Follow your interests and passions. Listen to your inner voice. Trust yourself. Your intuition is rarely wrong.

—CHAPTER 6—

PASSION

SYLVIA EARLE, PH.D.

Why do so many people lose their fervor during the course of life? Do you ever feel like all your energy has been taken away? Does life seem tedious and pointless from time to time? How do you remain passionate over the years?

Dr. Sylvia Earle is arguably the most famous marine biologist in the world. Through her tireless research, she has achieved many breakthroughs in her field, including the discovery of numerous forms of sea life. Sylvia is also an acclaimed explorer, who has set world records for independently exploring the great depths of the ocean. She has spent more time underwater than just about any living human being, almost a full year of accumulated diving time. At one point, she lived underwater in an ocean research habitat for two weeks. This 1970's research project, called Tektite II, made Sylvia a leading symbol of women's equality during the sexual revolution. She has led over fifty expeditions and is currently the author of approximately 125 scientific and popular publications. Among her many honors, Sylvia has been inducted into the National Women's Hall of Fame.

Today Sylvia owns and operates a company called DOER Marine, which is involved in ocean exploration and research. With its groundbreaking work in underwater robotics and submersibles, the company strives to use its state-of-the-art technology for positive educational and environmental purposes. In addition to her work with DOER, Sylvia spends her time as an explorer-in-residence for the National Geographic Society. Through the financial backing of this organization, she partakes in exciting expeditions all over the world. As if that's not enough, Sylvia is also one of the most powerful environmentalists in the country. She feels it is her responsibility to fight for the preservation of the environment and the maintenance of the nation's waters. At one point, she was even the chief scientist for the National Oceanographic and Atmospheric Administration. Although she no longer holds this position, Sylvia still influences many of the top political decision-makers in Washington D.C.

Throughout the years, Sylvia's parents, her three children, her grandchildren, and several close, devoted friends have been the most important priority in her life. She says that all her accomplishments mean very little without her family and friends. Sylvia lives in the foothills of Oakland, with her daughter Elizabeth, her son-in-law and two adorable grandchildren. Their home is on two and a half acres, completely secluded from the outside world. On the premises, they have two horses, ten chickens, a rooster, numerous tropical parrots, four dogs, three cats and a large goldfish pond. They also have a luscious fruit and vegetable garden, from which they eat every day. Their serene home feels like a magnificent blend of Noah's Arc and the Garden of Eden.

I met Sylvia at her home in Oakland, California:

Q: You've been able to do and accomplish so much in your life. In the early days of your career, did you conceive that you would be where you are today?

A: I'm not quite sure where I am today, but I always wanted to be a biologist, even when I didn't know what to call it. I knew I wanted to be a scientist.

Q: How did you decide to become a marine biologist?

A: I didn't decide; it just happened. I fell in love with the ocean when I was about three years old. I got knocked over by a wave, the ocean got my attention, and life in the ocean has held my attention ever since. There was just no question that that was what I was going to do.

Q: How were you able to be successful in so many various arenas? You're a marine biologist, scientist, explorer, world-record holder, environmentalist…the list continues.

A: Well, anybody can do this; it's just a matter of not allowing yourself to get boxed in. There are a thousand people who will tell you that you can't do something, but you just have to do what you know you have to do. Go around the walls, over the walls, under the walls or through the walls. Just figure out ways to get where you want to go. A lot of people seem to just be constrained by the belief that they can't do it.

Q: When you became a marine biologist, you were one of the only women in the field early on. Did you have to break through a lot of social barriers?

A: I wasn't trying to break any barriers. I was just doing what I wanted to do. It didn't matter to me whether there were other women in the classes that I took or not; that was truly incidental. I wanted to do what I wanted to do. [Laughing] It was an issue with others, but it certainly was not an issue with me.

Q: Many of the things that you've accomplished in your life involve risk. You set a world record for diving in the greatest depths of the ocean.

A: Yes, but think about driving in traffic. You're separated from oncoming cars by nothing more than your goodwill and a painted yellow line. That's dangerous; that really is scary.

Q: Is the risk less daunting because you are following your passion?

A: Yes, I mean truly. I'll take calculated risks, but I won't take foolish risks. I try to control the risky things. You go over everything with as much detail as you can and then you sort of put all that behind you and get on with doing what you're there to do. The biggest threat under water is panic.

Q: How did you find the career that you were passionate about? Is it serendipity or is it something you have to look for?

A: I don't know. I wish I could answer that. If I could get people's recipe for finding their individual passion, I'd share it with the world. [Laughing] I suggest that they make a career out of what they really love.

Q: Does fate play a part in that?

A: I think I would have been a scientist no matter what. I think I would have been led to the ocean no matter what.

Q: So you definitely feel like we have control over our destinies?

A: I think that we do, but I also think that we're born with certain attributes that lead us in a certain direction. You've got certain inherent talents. If you're good at something, that tends to be the way life takes you.

Q: It seems like once you have a thought in your mind, you make it happen.

A: Well, why not? People have that power. That's a great thing about being a human being. We're not in a cage. If we were in a cage, then there would be an excuse.

Q: Have you always been so attuned to what you want out of life?

A: Well, it makes you a bit of a maverick. Of course in order to live in civilized society you've got to abide by the general rules of civil behavior. [Laughing] So I try not to do stupid things. Well, I can't say that's always true.

Q: Once you knew what you wanted, did you have to make sacrifices in order to achieve it?

A: You have to make choices. There are only so many things that you can accomplish. I missed being with my mother all the time in her later years when she was without health; you have to make some tough decisions. But it wouldn't have been good for either of us if I had chosen to not do some of the other things that I did do, and in fact, I had to make a living to earn the money, so that she could have the care she needed and keep the home that she loved. With a lot of things, you have to strike a balance.

Q: But throughout your life, has family been an anchor for you?

A: Critical, yes. They've been there as an anchor for me and I've tried to be an anchor for them.

Q: What qualities do you think have helped you become accomplished in your field?

A: Curiosity, being willing to always ask questions—that's what kids do. Some people ask, "How did you get to be an explorer?" I say, "It's really easy, you start out as a kid, and you do what kids do. Keep asking questions—who, what, why, how, where—and you never stop, just keep doing it." So it's that attitude of never being quite content that this is all there is. Keep saying, "Well, what else is there?" [Laughing]

Q: What does it take to be a visionary?

A: Opening your eyes. [Laughing] It's looking, not just at where you are today but where you're going to be.

Q: What do you look forward to in your future?

A: I'm less driven than some by a need to make sure that I have a secure, big bank account. I discovered that what you have in terms of personal possessions, even your house, is vulnerable. So you have to invest in yourself, and mostly in your mind. Learn as much as you can, read everything that you can and pack in personal experiences as much as you can. It's the only insurance that really does matter.

Q: With all your research, you spend a lot of time alone. Do you need to be independent in life?

A: I enjoy being alone, but I also love being with people. I don't panic at the thought of traveling around the world by myself or going to the bottom of the ocean by myself or taking on a new project on my own without a lot of help. The world is what it is because individuals have chosen to do things on their own.

Q: What does it take to build a great team around you?

A: Great people! [Laughing] I try to empower the people around me. We are always working together to make something happen. I love to empower other people. It gives me just such a kick to see the light in their eyes.

Q: How crucial is it to keep hope and be an optimist?

A: It's absolutely vital. Without hope we're back to what drives people to be terrorists—desperation, lack of hope, lack of anticipating a future where you can see yourself and your family.

Q: What's the value of being a dreamer?

A: It's what makes the world go around. Many of the great accomplishments of technology and science start with a vision. There are people that dreamed of going to the moon long before we had the technology in hand to make that possible. It starts with an idea.

Q: How would you advise other people to become successful in their own lives?

A: Be as knowledgeable as you can, be a voracious reader and be a sponge in terms of gathering information. Invest in your good brain. [Laughing] Everyone has more brain than they actually ever use. [Laughing] And don't give up, don't get soft and think that there's no hope.

Q: Keep fighting during bad times?

A: Absolutely! Keep looking over the horizon. You owe it not so much to yourself as to others. One of the great things about being a human being is that we're all connected. We're connected to the past, we're connected to the present and we're certainly connected to the future. So we almost have an obligation not to let ourselves wallow in self-pity.

Q: Would you say you have a faith in the world?

A: A faith in the good. I want this generation to be remembered as the time when things turned around and that we got it.

Q: What would you say is the secret to happiness and fulfillment in your life?

A: Isn't that the great mystery of life? What is the secret of happiness? [Laughing] Doing the best that you can to achieve the goals you've set out for yourself. I'm happy when I make somebody else happy. I'm happy when I give an earthworm a chance to live, when it's crawling across the sidewalk, and I manage to turn it around. I'm happy when I think I've been able to make a difference in a positive sort of way. I'm happy when I get a job done. I'm just happy when I have time with the kids, seeing them learn something.

Q: What aspects about society fill you with the greatest hope?

A: I see the goodwill on the part of people everyday. It dominates! On the whole, there's good reason to believe that people, if they know what the right thing to do is, will opt in that direction. Ignorance is the biggest problem; they don't always know the right thing to do. Our greatest hope for peace is understanding and knowledge, (so that) we will put ourselves in the place of others and wish them well.

Q: So despite some of the problems, society has a lot of positive elements?

A: Definitely! Even consider that all of us live like kings in a sense, as compared to our predecessors, even those of very modest means by today's standards. Think about the availability of water, clothing, transportation, places to live, rights and freedoms, especially that, opportunities to take your life in your own hands and do something with it. Whatever it is, with all of its soft spots and problems, there's no better place in the world than this country and there's no better time to be in this world than now.

Q: What do you think our greatest challenge is today?

A: The direction that we're going in with respect to the natural world has been a great concern to me. We do not have as much regard as we should for other creatures. We need to make our peace with the environment. We need to stabilize this catastrophic slide into the unsustainable use of the world around us. If we continue on the path that our predecessors embarked upon from ten thousand years ago to the present, we will do what bacteria in a dish will do. They consume the world around them and then they die. I don't want that to happen to us. We have the power. We have the knowledge. We have the means to find that wonderful relationship with the natural world. But that's the biggest challenge, the greatest challenge that faces human kind.

Q: Has conservation motivated you throughout the years?

A: Absolutely, it drives me. Out of all the creatures on the earth, I love human beings the most; there's no question of that. I am a certifiable tree-hugger, a whale-hugger, fish-hugger, you name it, but people are what I care about most of all. It is incredible to me that everyone doesn't see the connections between human beings and the natural world. We're totally dependent on maintaining the integrity of our system; it provides what we need.

Q: What would you tell other people to do to help the environment?

A: Well, first to become informed; ignorance is the biggest threat. We really need to understand first that we are connected to nature; we have to protect the systems that protect us. We've got to take care of it, and it isn't just because we think bears are cute or that trees are nice. It's because we are absolutely dependent on it. Collapse the natural environment, and the civilization around it disappears.

Q: Sylvia, how urgent is this?

A: Extremely urgent! I mean this is the highest priority. What I find perplexing is why it's so difficult for many people to make a connection between sound environment and sound economy; they are not total opposites, the way many people seem to conclude. You cannot have a prosperous economy without a prosperous, healthy ecosystem to support it.

Q: Long-term?

A: Absolutely, you can get away with some pretty awful things for a short time but not for a lifetime.

Q: So what do you think needs to change?

A: Knowledge is the key. We need to have a much better informed public.

Q: Are there any other actions we can take to start helping the environment?

A: Well, knowledge will lead you to some pretty obvious conclusions, including that you have got to take care of the systems that take care of you. Less obvious and therefore more dangerous in many ways is what's happening to the ocean. We're doing to the ocean what we did to big wildlife on land. We really need to stop, and I don't mean just cut back. Commercial fishing is destroying the underpinnings of what makes the ocean function.

Q: Where do you think we'll be thirty years from now?

A: Well, it could go either way. My dream is that we will see a turning toward responsible behavior with respect to one another and with respect to the living world around us.

Q: So you're optimistic?

A: I have to be, I want to be and I guess I am. [Laughing] There are lots of reasons why I'm inspired to think this could work.

Q: How do you want to be remembered in your life and in your work?

A: I'd like to be remembered as positively as my mom and dad were remembered; as people who cared about those around them. As somebody who left the world a little better than I found it; I'd like to make it a lot better. I'll do the best I can. It's something to aspire to anyway.

Talking with Sylvia Earle, it is easy to become inspired by her passion, which is demonstrated by her love of people, family, human nature, animals, the environment, science and exploration—the list is inexhaustible. Sylvia approaches life from the heart, with optimism, energy and conviction. She celebrates her existence by living every day to the fullest, and believing that dreams can come true.

Sylvia's fervor reminds us what a privilege it is to be on this earth! To dream at night, breathe fresh air and observe a beautiful sunset. To raise a family, cherish friends and find love. To help others and make a positive difference. These are just some of the gifts and opportunities each one of us has every single day. Having passion is about being grateful for the simple things in life.

Many of us lose passion because we experience various disappointments. We make a few wrong choices and start feeling trapped. We grow cynical after being burned one too many times, and decide to compromise our dreams. There is no question that life has its share of trials and tribulations. However, what makes life so amazing is the fact that the good is always mixed in with the bad. We have sadness and we have hope, failure and success, greed and charity, illness and recovery, hatred and love. Without the bad parts of life, it would be so difficult to embrace the good parts. In spite of our struggles, it's up to each one of us to seek out the good. That is true passion!

—Chapter 7—

Optimism

Wally Amos

When faced with failure and misfortune, how do you keep your head up? Why should we think that tomorrow will bring a better day? What's the point of being optimistic?

Wally Amos is best known for being the founder of Famous Amos Cookies. In 1975, he opened his first cookie store in Los Angeles, California. Over time, Famous Amos became one of the largest cookie brands in the world. The success of Famous Amos inspired the gourmet cookie trend that later included companies such as Mrs. Fields. Today, Wally remains a national spokesman for Famous Amos Cookies, and is also the owner of Uncle Wally's Muffins and Aunt Della's Cookies, nationally recognized brands independent from his original company.

Wally has had to overcome adversity throughout his life. From growing up in a broken home, to witnessing segregation as a child, to dropping out of high school, to being sued by unscrupulous business associates, Wally has never had it easy. At one time, because of a lawsuit, he couldn't even use his own name in his business. However, as a result of his work ethic and positive attitude, he has never allowed adversity to hold him back. In addition to his business success, Wally has become an acclaimed philanthropist. Once a high-school dropout, he has become one of the most dedicated supporters of literacy and education in the country. Moreover, he has been a sought-after motivational speaker hired by Fortune 500 corporations. Wally is also an accomplished author, who has written five books about life philosophy and inspiration.

Wally has been happily married to his wife Christine for the last twenty-five years. He credits his successful marriage to a strong foundation of faith and true friendship. The couple lives in beautiful Lanikai, Hawaii, only two blocks from one of the most breathtaking beaches in the world. Meeting Wally, you are struck by his ever-present smile. His good spirit is so infectious that you can't help but feel joy in his company.

I met Wally at his home in Lanikai, Hawaii:

Q: Do you feel that you're extraordinary?

A: We're all ordinary people doing extraordinary things. That's what it is. That's where the link is. If the average reader sees these people as being extraordinary and superhuman, then they would look at themselves and say, "Wow, I could never do that." The idea is to show them the commonality, how they have the same qualities that a successful person has. I tell people if I could do it, anybody could do it. I'm a high school dropout.

Q: How does a person learn what it takes to lead an extraordinary life?

A: I think the best way is through experience. Each of us brings our own personality, attitude and skills. People ask, "What's the secret?" The secret is there is no secret. Besides, I'm never attempting to achieve extraordinary things; I'm just looking to get through each day. I'm just looking to be successful and set goals. What can I do each day?

Q: What do you believe is the biggest reason that you have had such success in your life?

A: Because I wanted to succeed. I believed that I could and success followed that. Results follow belief. Results follow action.

Q: What other qualities have led to your success?

A: I think it's very basic. Attitude! If you don't have a good attitude, then nobody will want to be around you. It's your attitude that creates your reality. It's your attitude that attracts people. But then again, I think it's important to understand that success is different for everybody. It's very individual, so you have to first define success for yourself. Don't let other people define you!

Q: Does success come from valuing your life and not taking the opportunities in your life for granted?

A: This is all that you have, as far as you know. Why would you throw it away? Why would you be disrespectful of it? Why wouldn't you want to make the very best of this life? Just to have the satisfaction that you made a difference, that you made a contribution. That is what will give you satisfaction.

Q: What kind of thought process has led to your great business ideas?

A: I don't even know the unconscious thought process. The thing that I've come to rely on is divine intervention and divine guidance. I don't believe that answers come from me. I believe that answers come through me, that ideas are from God. I think answers are always coming and if you're in tune and you're listening, then you'll see them.

Q: What does it take to be an entrepreneur or revolutionary thinker? Does an entrepreneur have vision?

A: Absolutely, he sees beyond the numbers. An entrepreneur looks at the opportunity and says, "Wow this is great, I don't care what it takes to do this, but I'm going to do this. I'm going to make this happen." Sometimes what counts can't be counted, and what's counted doesn't count. [Laughing] That's what an entrepreneur does. He sees the intangible, and he's able to take it and make something with it.

Q: What if people try to discourage you along the way?

A: Cynics are just negative people. Cynics never create anything. Cynics just tell you what you can't do. Cynics condemn and criticize, but cynics never come up with a creative idea.

Q: What's the secret to finding the kind of work that you love, and why doesn't it happen to more people?

A: Well, I think most people are not able to because they believe that it's not possible. They're also so focused on making money. I think if you do what you love to do then ultimately the money will come. Even if the money doesn't come, as long as you can make a living doing it, as long as you can provide for yourself, then you get the inner satisfaction of doing what you love to do. I know too many people that make tons and tons of money that are miserable. They're just caught up in their cycle of making more money, simply to make more money. I mean after a point, why? What do you do with more money? It's a very hollow, very empty feeling. So it is important to find something that you really love and something that you connect to on a deeper level and pursue that.

Q: Do you believe that our society places too much emphasis on money?

A: Oh, without a doubt, no question! That's it. They'll kill for it; they'll cheat, steal and lie. [Laughing]

Q: So let's talk a little more about your personality characteristics. How essential is self-awareness?

A: I think self-awareness is very essential. Being aware of my actions, being aware of how I respond to people and being aware of my thoughts. I think watching yourself is really important. How do you respond to life? How do you respond to people? What are your thoughts? What are your habits? You can't improve yourself if you can't change your negative habits. You have to be aware that you have them.

Q: How important is teamwork, the ability to work with other people?

A: It's critical in order to succeed, because the only thing that you can do by yourself is fail. In order to do anything, you're going to need somebody else. There are no self-made people except alcoholics. I think you have to acknowledge other people and their contribution to the team. There is no limit to what can be accomplished if it doesn't matter who gets the credit. If all you want is the glory and the credit, then you're going to alienate the rest of the team and no one will want to be there with you. It's really about acknowledging other people in your life. It's about praising them, complementing them and rewarding them. Everyone wants to feel special. Whatever you give to somebody else will ultimately be returned to you tenfold.

Q: What's the value of being a dreamer in life?

A: What else has value? [Laughing] If you're not a dreamer, then where do you go? What do you do? Where do you get ideas? It's all a dream anyways. [Laughing] It's all made up. [Laughing]

Q: What's the secret to staying passionate over the years?

A: If you're not passionate how can you survive? How can you get up? How can you do anything with any feeling, with any success?

Q: What's the significance of failing and making mistakes along the way? How do you recover from some of those failures?

A: I don't believe in failure. [Laughing] Most things that you do in life, you do for the first time. You're usually attempting to do something that you've never done. How can you fail? You have no practice at it. You've never done it before. How can you be a failure? That's the way you learn. Realize that there is no failure, make the best of it, keep going and do it again.

Q: How essential is an ability to take risks?

A: I've got a viewpoint on that. Everything is a risk. Tell me one thing that's a sure shot, a guarantee.

Q: Sitting on your couch at home.

A: But you could die. You could fall off the couch and break your arm. A picture could fall from the wall and hit you in the head. It's all a risk. So to think about risk I believe is living life from a negative perspective. I'm positive. I think about succeeding. Of course, I know that unless I do something I will not succeed. [Laughing] But there is nothing to fear. What you fear, you create. You're making it all up.

Q: How large of a role has faith played in your life?

A: There's a quote that I say in the morning at the end of my prayer time: "God, take me where you want me to go today, let me meet who you want me to meet today, tell me what you want me to say today, and please keep me out of the way." I just want to follow God's guidance. I heard a minister friend of mine, a Baptist minister in D.C. who has long since passed away, but he said something that will stick with me. He said, "The only reason that we exist is to serve one another." I have yet to come up with a better reason for breathing.

Q: When everything seems bad, how do you spend your time in

order to rejuvenate your spirits?

A: Well, it never seems that bad. My spirit doesn't necessarily need rejuvenating. [Laughing]

Q: I think a lot of people wish they had that kind of attitude.

A: It takes work to have that. You can't go through life sleeping; you got to wake up. You have to be aware about what's going on.

Q: On a more personal note, growing up, your family struggled. How did this affect you? Did it have an impact on your future thinking?

A: Of course it did. I was born in Tallahassee, Florida during segregation in 1936. Segregation in the South was in full force, where blacks had no rights. Seeing that as a little kid growing up affected my thinking for many, many years to come. My mother and father were illiterate; books were not a part of my early life. Yet, I would become one of the biggest advocates for reading as an adult. That's life! There are hundreds of ironies throughout everybody's life. You are affected by your environment and by your childhood, but there's also always a possibility to break out of the negative.

Q: How do you break out of the negative cycle?

A: I've looked at that a lot, and I don't have a formula. The one thing that I've always had is my work ethic, and I think that has been really important.

Q: What kind of conclusions did you make later on in your life about the discrimination that you saw as a child?

A: As I got older, I learned that the color of my skin is just the color of my skin. My veins are not black. I don't have a black soul. I don't have a black heart. The color of my skin does not affect the way that I think. I've learned to respect me. I've learned that I'm important. I've learned that I'm special. The more I learn about me, the better I'm able to respond to others.

Q: After all your amazing experiences, what do you have the greatest love for in your life?

A: Life, breathing. [Laughing] The most important part of life is breathing. [Laughing] If you can breathe, then you can put the rest of it together. When you can't breath, everything else is gone. I just want to keep breathing, one breath at a time.

Q: Do you feel that your positive attitude in your own life is reflected in society? What aspects about our society fill you with hope?

A: I'm hopeful because I believe that life is a positive experience. I believe that life is ever-renewing. It's always moving forward.

Q: What are the biggest problems that our society faces?

A: It's not just American society, it's the planet. We're not loving enough to one another. We treat each other so badly. I am amazed at our capacity to be mean to one another, downright nasty. I'm absolutely amazed at how we can do the things we do to other human beings.

Q: If you had the power to change one thing about the world, what would it be?

A: You only see what you project. We're all projectors. We are constantly projecting our ways onto the world. So if I could help everyone see themselves in a more positive light, then they would see everyone else in a positive light. I think many of our minor grievances, problems and insecurities would disappear.

Q: So after everything is said and done, what do you believe is the meaning of life?

A: I think the meaning of life is to love one another. Learning to love life for life rather than for all the material things. Believing in the inherent goodness of one another. Believing in love. Believing in something bigger than yourself.

Q: How do you want to be remembered?

A: I would want to be remembered as a guy who cared about other people, who shared his love. Wally Amos, he really was a nice guy. He was a good person. He was a kind person. He was a loving person.

Wally is always optimistic. Even during difficult times, he never loses hope. He believes that everything is possible with the right attitude. There are no limitations or boundaries when you believe in yourself. Never let anyone tell you that you can't do something. Cynics are just negative, insecure people who feel poorly about their own lives. Instead of listening to negative opinions, determine for yourself what is possible. Often times, you will be surprised how much strength and ability you really have.

Wally's optimism has been a major reason behind his success. He sees the best in every situation, and takes the rest in stride. In fact, Wally doesn't believe in failure. He views setbacks and mistakes as mere steps along the road to success. If you try and fail, do not turn against yourself and give in to negative energy. Just think about how you can do the same thing better next time. Eventually, you'll get to where you want to be.

Having a positive attitude makes you a happier person. It makes you pleasant to be around. It gives you strength, energy and passion. It encourages you to try hard and never give up. As long as you're doing your absolute best, there is no reason not to be optimistic about the future. Wally's life demonstrates that attitude plays a role in making destiny. Optimism results in a self-fulfilling prophecy. If you think you'll fail, you'll fail. If you think you'll succeed, you'll succeed. Each one of us is offered the choice. Which one do you want?

—CHAPTER 8—

EMPATHY

ROBERT DENNARD, PH.D.

Why do we react negatively at times to people we view as being different from ourselves? Why do we feel like we have to convince others to be more like us? Why can't we be more respectful, understanding and compassionate towards one another?

In 1968, while working for IBM, Dr. Robert "Bob" Dennard attended a seminar hosted by some colleagues. They were working on computer memory using existing technology, which was slow and inefficient. Bob felt that their efforts were misdirected. Over the next several months, with a lot of trial and error, Bob found a way to build a simplified, more effective computer chip. The result was Dynamic Random Access Memory, or RAM, the technology that is used to this day for all the digital circuitry in computers, including memory chips like the Intel Pentium Processor. Before Bob's breakthrough, computers were complex, enormous and unaffordable. The new memory chip changed all that and helped inspire the computer revolution.

Since his world-changing innovation, Bob has spent his career improving this technology. His work's impact on the computer industry, and consequently on our society, is universally recognized. To this day, he is considered one of the foremost computer experts in the world. Among his many honors, he was awarded the prestigious title of Fellow at IBM, inducted into the National Inventors Hall of Fame and presented the National Medal of Technology by the President of the United States.

Bob has a Ph.D. in Electrical Engineering from the Carnegie Institute of Technology. He has been working at the IBM Watson Research Center in Yorktown, New York for almost forty-five years. In his personal life, Bob is happily married to his loving wife Jane. They met each other in a Scottish country dancing class. They are good friends that share many common interests including art, music, sports and, of course, dancing. He speaks of her with much gratitude and affection.

I met Bob at the IBM Watson Research Center in Yorktown Heights, New York:

Q: In the early days of your research, did you conceive of the impact that your work would eventually have on the world?

A: I guess we really didn't conceive how much the world of computing would change and how much that would change society as a result.

Q: What does it take to be an inventor or revolutionary thinker?

A: I've done some writing and some thinking about that. I finally decided that attitude is the most important thing, the attitude that you can do it. Invention is done by people…ordinary people.

Q: How do you realize which path to take in life and what you really want to do?

A: I suppose you can try them out and see what works. In my career, I have always made the best choice at the time, but that doesn't always happen in my personal life. [Laughing] I have chosen some bad relationships and then repeatedly chosen the same bad relationships. But anyway, I'm happy now. Those kinds of choices are really tough, who you're going to spend your time with. Choosing your relationships is very important.

Q: Are you one to follow your heart or your mind?

A: I try to listen to both actually. It's quite useful sometimes to think about what you really want to do rather than worry so much about why I should do this or that.

Q: Doesn't that require self-awareness, knowing who you are as a person and what you want out of life?

A: I never think much about that. I know who I am as a person. I know it's important for me to look in the mirror quite often, if that's what you mean by self-awareness. I look in the mirror and say, "That's me. I really exist. It's more than just a thought process. I'm also a person. I look like this. Maybe I can see some signs of aging, but basically it's the same thing that I've been all my life." That's a kind of self-awareness (that is) important to a person who spends a lot of time thinking.

Q: Once you decide what you want, how do you go from thinking about it to putting it into action?

A: It's a matter of being responsible. You just don't get anywhere unless you really go out and do the things you have to do. It's not always easy.

Q: How would you advise other people, especially young people, to become successful in achieving what they want in life?

A: Attitude is everything.

Q: And what kind of attitude?

A: Just a positive attitude, that in fact you can change the world.

Q: Has fate played a role in your success?

A: Part of fate is being healthy and surviving, not getting killed in some auto wreck.

Q: That we don't have control over.

A: Well, it's fate.

Q: What's the secret to being happy and fulfilled in life?

A: I don't feel I have any secret. I don't think it's a secret. I'm willing to share it with anyone. [Laughing] I guess the real secret is kind of what we talked about. If you do the right things, you will succeed and then you probably will be happy.

Q: While you were growing up your family struggled financially during the Great Depression. What kind of impact did this have on you for the rest of your life?

A: I think it probably led me to be an engineer and to have a pretty good career that I could depend on.

Q: Did it lead you to work harder?

A: Possibly. I certainly had a goal of becoming financially self-sufficient. I looked forward to the possibility. I figured that some day I would be called upon to support my parents in their older age.

Q: There was a sense of responsibility?

A: Yes. I certainly was motivated to succeed so my parents would be financially secure, and then maybe they would be proud of me as an unexpected bonus.

Q: What is the value of education and what kind of doors did it open for you in life?

A: It depends. I think everyone should have a right to a good liberal education. The more we know about the world, ourselves and our environment, the better. To some extent we need all that information just to be good citizens. Lack of education is probably one of the real threats to the future of society. However, I don't think we need a world totally full of lawyers and computer scientists.

Q: What do we need more of?

A: We need more plumbers, carpenters and plasterers. There are lots of places in society for people to be nurses, teachers…but unfortunately, the public in general doesn't place a lot of value in those things.

Q: We only value the professions where people make a lot of money?

A: Yes, and that's just totally wrong.

Q: What were your goals early in life? Did you always want to revolutionize science?

A: I just wanted to get out and not be a farmer. [Laughing]

Q: Besides avoiding a career in agriculture, what else motivates you in your life? Is it glory, other people, family, yourself?

A: I guess myself and my family. It's not glory. I haven't aspired for that, but I recognized it when the chance arose.

Q: When your spirits need rejuvenation, what are your favorite things to do?

A: Wait until the next day (when) the sun comes out again. I don't really enjoy much solitary time. I enjoy people. I enjoy seeing my dogs. Being around the yard brings me a good feeling. Good hard exercise is always important.

Q: What were the most difficult struggles you've had to overcome throughout your life?

A: Clearly, social and family situations. I had a son who had a brain tumor.

Q: That's unimaginable. What can you do to keep yourself on your feet, when you're subjected to something like that?

A: Use all the resources available to you. Take advantage of all your friendships. In times of distress, you cannot be isolated; that's the main thing. You have to get out there and find whatever it is that people are offering that will help you with your struggle. There are a lot of people willing to help. There are a lot of people in the same situation.

Q: After going through something horrible like that, how do you pick yourself up and continue living your life?

A: Well, first of all you're stronger. Dealing with these problems makes you develop all these traits that you never had before. So you are stronger.

Q: Does it cause you to reprioritize, and look at life in a different way?

A: Yes, I think so. I've learned the value of a good, stable family life and what it takes to have one. It's give and take.

Q: After your family, what has given you the greatest satisfaction in your life?

A: At some stage, I don't know if it's easy to explain, but I did begin to feel comfortable with myself and secure (with what) I had achieved. I think having a successful career. Also, somehow getting through all my personal family problems and getting back the feeling that I was in control of myself.

Q: What do you think are the biggest problems we face as a society today?

A: I think that in general we have a lack of leadership—a very big lack of leadership. That's what annoys me. I don't think our leaders lead. They just manage to keep the existence going. They don't provide any moral leadership. They don't set any goals in this regard.

Q: How can we change this?

A: Well, there's one thing that I believe very strongly, people do make a difference to the world. If you find something broken, it's up to you to fix it. There are lots of things broken. If there's something in the road, don't just go around it. Get it off the road so that the next person doesn't have to face that problem. You know, that's not the prevailing attitude, not at all.

Q: What do you think is the major purpose behind our society now? Is purpose something that we need to discuss more often?

A: Yes. [Laughing] We don't talk about that very much. We don't talk about what's important. I think that the long-term survival of the universe should be one of those things that we should consider. That would motivate me a lot.

Q: If you had the power to change one thing about the world, what would it be?

A: I guess I would be very careful about exercising any such power. If you're literally saying I had the power, I would probably not like to have such power. I don't know that I have the true answer because obviously there's such a diversity of opinions about everything.

Q: Is there something that would benefit everybody?

A: You mean like wiping out the common cold. [Laughing] Yes, that would benefit everybody. If I could also take away all the allergies in the world, that would be really great. (Allergies) really bother me; they are one of the most annoying things that I have to deal with. [Laughing]

Q: When it is all said and done, how do you want to be remembered?

A: I haven't thought about that very much. My love and respect for other people—I'm pretty proud of that but it's nothing I'll be remembered for because nobody particularly realizes it. People close to me probably do. Yes, they might remember me for that; they might very well. My wife seems to like me. I don't always listen to her as well as I should, but she seems to like me. There's something basic about me that she seems to like. That's probably what I'll be remembered for.

Bob is a very gentle, kind and caring person. He has a respect for other people and a compassion for their feelings. Bob realizes that people are different; they have their own opinions and ways to approach life. He does not assume to know the answers for everyone. He strongly believes that people should be equally appreciated no matter what they do. How much money a person makes does not determine their value. Individuals should only be judged as to whether they are good, honest human beings.

To a certain degree, his compassion for others stems from his personal struggles. After two painful divorces and a son's losing fight with a brain tumor, Bob has made some hard conclusions about life. He believes that we don't pay enough attention to one another; we don't support each other properly in dealing with the pressures that we all undergo. It's unfortunate, because we all face the same sorts of issues. It's part of the human condition.

Some people may ask why it's important to have empathy. How does it benefit them? For one, people tend to treat you the same way you treat them. If you do not show compassion for others, a time will come when you will end up alone and unhappy. Having compassion is about being a good person. It's about valuing human life and wanting to make a difference. In society, there's so much hatred, misunderstanding, discrimination and disrespect, all for what reason? If we had more empathy for one another, many of our problems would be solved. We would live in a better, safer world. Isn't that something we all should aspire to?

—Chapter 9—

Teamwork

Charito Kruvant

Do we need other people in order to achieve what we want in life? What does it take to be able to work with other people?

Charito Kruvant is the majority owner, president and CEO of Creative Associates, a Washington D.C. company that she started in 1977. Today, this privately-owned organization employs approximately 200 employees, produces revenues of over $60 million a year, and has offices around the world including Guatemala, El Salvador, South Africa, Angola, Jordan, Lebanon and Afghanistan. Among other things, Creative Associates assists developing countries in the implementation of infrastructure and offers issue-resolution for a wide array of social, political and economic problems. Recently, Creative Associates has helped rebuild the educational system in Afghanistan and Iraq after the military operations. In the past, Charito's company has had many remarkable projects, including helping South Africa end Apartheid.

Raised in Bolivia and Argentina, Charito moved to the United States in her early twenties. Despite being a first-generation immigrant and a woman, she was able to build a large business in the male-dominated political arena of Washington D.C. Overcoming great odds, she has spent the last thirty years confronting problems around the world. It is truly her life's work. Charito holds a Masters in Early Childhood Development from the University of Maryland, and says her work with children remains most important to her.

At the age of fifteen, Charito met her future husband during a foreign exchange program to the United States. After five years of dating, they married on New Years Eve, 1966. Despite different religions and nationalities, they remain together to this day, and have raised two wonderful children, proving that true love conquers all. Charito speaks about her husband and children with devotion, care and admiration. However demanding her business may be, Charito has always made family her number one priority in life.

I met Charito at Creative Associates headquarters in Washington D.C.:

Q: What were your original intentions and goals for your career?

A: I wanted to help myself and help others. Not just one or two, but help the community at large.

Q: You wanted to make a difference?

A: From way, way back. I can remember being five or six and knowing that I have to be responsible. I'm always like that. I have big shoulders, and I think it's because God gave me that opportunity to look after others. People can lean on my shoulders.

Q: When you were getting your masters degree in child development, were you thinking, "I'm going to start a business"?

A: When I had the degree, I understood that to be the best day care director, I would make thirteen thousand dollars. Deep inside, what I said to myself was, "I could make enough money doing something else to be able to donate thirteen thousand dollars every single year." It's the whole issue of opportunity cost. I'm always good at that, sorting out where to spend most of my energy to have the best impact.

Q: How did you actually conceive of the idea for your business? Was it an epiphany?

A: No, it was more of an evolution I think. The idea of self-sufficiency was always a big issue for me. Having economic security was also of importance. The idea of (women) being paid for our services in an equitable manner was also important. I've also always been very clear about having enough for myself. I don't shy away from beautiful things—beautiful flowers, beautiful painting.

Q: How have you been able to overcome obstacles along the way?

A: I'm hard on myself. I don't apologize. Life is tough, so what? I've always known that I had to work a little harder than others.

Q: It doesn't discourage you?

A: No, it has always allowed me to learn. I know I need to be part of a team. I value that and so I always find myself with the best team I could possibly have. I know that I don't succeed alone. I'm nobody unless I'm part of a larger team.

Q: Through your work, you help millions of people. Does that greater purpose keep motivating you through the years?

A: You know, sometimes in the morning, I pray to have the wisdom, ability and clarity to support others. If something is not done as well as it can possibly be done, then someone could get hurt. So you keep at it, doing the very best you can.

Q: They say great people are the product of great parents. Did you have very supportive parents?

A: Yes, they were very special people. The family was an environment where we spent lots of time. We always had these long tables with lots of family and friends telling stories. This whole issue of being part of a larger world was always there. It was a big issue for both my parents. They always made us feel a bigger responsibility towards others. There were always others who needed more.

Q: Did they make you feel really special? Is that why you possibly felt a special responsibility to the greater world?

A: Yes. I was special, and when you're special you're responsible for others. I was very, very dark always, much darker than the rest of my family, but I had a sense of beauty. [Laughing] I had this very special feeling that I was beautiful. Argentina was a very, very white European world; they reminded you that you were dark, constantly. I was the darkest one in the school, but my Father used to say that it was a positive attribute—my dark skin with my very, very white teeth. I was beautiful. [Laughing]

Q: Beyond your family life, were there any significant events that impacted you during your childhood?

A: When I was twelve or thirteen, I went to the Chaco region in the tropics on the border of Brazil and Argentina to do inoculations for children in extreme poverty. I remember having that sense of more than joy, like you're doing something special.

Q: What goals did you have early on in your life?

A: Success for me is still very much family-oriented, the idea of having a happy and healthy life within the family. The idea of being able to be of help is also important. The ability to travel and to see other parts of the world is important. I always thought what a wonderful life it would be to travel.

Q: So your success in business would not have mattered nearly as much if you didn't have the family?

A: I had many friends, many women friends at different stages in my life. They chose to do whatever they thought better at work and gave up their family life. I was sorry for them, and in the long run, I'm sure that society didn't benefit them much by having a successful business without a family.

Q: So family has been your most important ambition in life?

A: It has been crucial. The idea that you're not alone is important and the idea that you're responsible for somebody else's life. When we were married, there were a lot of cross-cultural issues. (People said) that we're not going to make it as a couple.

Q: Because your husband was American?

A: Yes, and I was Christian and he was Jewish. So the assumption was that we weren't going to make it. So some of what I wanted to show, to myself and to others, was that this is really important to me.

Q: You and your husband have obviously been able to overcome all your differences.

A: Bill and I were very lucky, but Bill and I were also disciplined at wanting to be together. I have great admiration for him; he's totally an intellectual guy. He's just so knowledgeable. But then Bill, as we get older, admires that I don't shy away from things. I just do it. If I make a mistake, I do it again.

Q: Has that perseverance helped you in your professional life? What are the qualities that have led to your career success?

A: I think straight-forwardness, a clear goal, perseverance and open, direct, clear communication. Also teamwork and respect for one another. The more we do that and the more we live with these values, the easier it becomes for us to go on the right track. Some of it is the idea, what am I good at? I think I'm good at pulling people together.

Q: What makes you such an effective leader? What qualities allow you to bring people together?

A: I think that the idea of being straightforward and honest is one (quality). The idea of needing other people is another, because you can't be a leader alone. To be a leader, you have to be willing to be of service, because you can't be a leader if you have not demonstrated that you can be of service to somebody else.

Q: How do you go from thinking about something to putting it into action?

A: Knowing the value of the team. Then having the discipline to do that what we committed ourselves to do.

Q: You risk your life with your work. You've been airlifted into areas of South America to negotiate with rebel guerrillas. How do you have the courage to do these things?

A: A lot of us want a lot, but need little. Either by ignorance, arrogance or by total knowledge that God will look out for me, I know that I will be okay today, tomorrow and as long as I live. I just know.

Q: What role has faith played in your life?

A: I'm totally convinced that there is a greater source.

Q: You seem to have such passion for everything you do. What's the secret to staying passionate about life?

A: I think just living the day, because the moment matters. I have these prayers, "I'm here and now. I'm happy and wholesome. I'm here for others." The other prayer is, "If I'm not for myself, who am

I? If I'm not for others, what am I?" So when you get confronted with options or day-to-day choices—don't do it just for yourself, do it for others.

Q: In your career, you devote much of your energy to solving disputes around the world. Are there any aspects of our society that fill you with hope?

A: I think that the young people are smart, and they also have good hearts. At the office here, we have a tremendous amount of young people that come, not because they want a big salary, but because they want to be content with themselves and also to do good things for others.

Q: What would you say are the biggest problems facing our society right now?

A: We want it right now—the shortness, the immediacy.

Q: Does American society suffer mostly from economic problems or spiritual problems?

A: Most of us in this society have a roof and something to eat. What we don't have is the assurance that we are part of a world and that we count.

Q: So is it almost like a feeling of being alone?

A: Yes, a feeling that I don't count. I think that sometimes, particularly young people, feel like, what's the purpose, it's not worth it. They don't pursue the opportunity to do more.

Q: How would you convince them to do more?

A: The more you give, the happier you are. We're all linked.

Q: If you had the power to change one thing about the world, what would it be?

A: Kids should be given the basics and the opportunity to do better. I don't think that kids in the world have that. I wish we could have a magic wand and make children be safe. Kids are not safe.

Q: So when everything is said and done, what do you believe is the meaning of life?

A: I think to do your best.

Q: How would you want to be remembered one day?

A: She was a good person. I want to be a good person. It's hard sometimes with the rush of doing fifty things. A good person has to put in the effort, energy and devotion.

Charito had three of her coworkers join our interview—right away, her concentration on teamwork was apparent. One of the most essential factors in Charito's success has been her ability to work with other people. She's not afraid to show her reliance on others and give them credit for their contributions. Her ability to communicate and understand others helps make her a great leader, capable of motivating a large number of people to achieve a common goal. Charito believes that multiple individuals working together can create something larger than the sum of their parts. Her emphasis on the value of teamwork is the secret of her success as a leader and a businesswoman.

Earlier in this book, Steve Wozniak showed us that independent thinking is essential. However, independent thinking does not eliminate the need for teamwork. No matter how strong we are as individuals, we will still need help from other people to achieve our dreams. Charito shows us that success is not defined by awards, accolades or money, but by the people in our lives. She understands that life would be barren without other people to provide us with the purpose and motivation to do our best.

—Chapter 10—

Fulfillment

Timothy Boyle

Do you appreciate what you have in life or do you always want more? Is the grass really greener on the other side? What brings happiness and self-fulfillment?

Timothy Boyle, the President and CEO of Columbia Sportswear, is a charismatic leader who built the company side-by-side with his mother. Their humorous relationship is reflected in a national advertising campaign in which a tough mother, Gertrude, is always disciplining her misbehaving son, Timothy. The Boyles caught my attention because they seemed like such humorous, good people. Besides, anyone who is able to work with his mother for thirty-three years and achieve such success must have some secrets to share.

In 1970, just as Timothy had finished college and was beginning to contemplate his future, his father died suddenly of a heart attack. Neal Boyle was not only a loving father and husband, but also the one who single-handedly operated Columbia Sportswear, their family business. His death left the company in shambles, with only Gertrude, a housewife, and Timothy, the oldest sibling, to get things in order. To make matters worse, the business possessed a large financial debt and was in danger of bankruptcy. The bankers were skeptical about the survival of the company and started pressuring the Boyles to sell. Sensing an opportunity, potential buyers offered the Boyles less than a few thousand dollars for the company. Courageously, Gertrude and Tim refused these offers, and vowed to keep the company afloat. That was over thirty-three years ago. Since that time, the dynamic duo has managed the company together. Today, Columbia Sportswear's market capitalization is over $2 billion, making the Boyles one of the wealthiest families in the United States.

Timothy married his wife Mary just before his father's passing. The Boyles have been together ever since and have two children. Timothy and Mary have had a successful family because they share a mutual love, understanding and commitment. Despite a demanding business schedule, they have both made family a top priority. The Boyles are frugal, humble and hard-working people who enjoy the simple things in life; acquiring their immense wealth has not changed who they are.

I met Tim at Columbia Sportswear headquarters in Portland, Oregon:

Q: How difficult was it for you when your father passed away in 1970? You were only twenty-one years old at the time, and you were forced into the family business.

A: It was probably more difficult than I knew at the time. It was all those things you don't really think about. This is going to be hard, but I guess I'm going to do it.

Q: Since that time, how have you been able to build such a large business?

A: It's just a lot of really terrific people that work here. There are a few overriding guidelines that we have, that allow for a tremendous amount of freedom and flexibility, emphasis on creativity, and a conservative financial model. For us, product is everything, and the creation of that product is key.

Q: What does it take to motivate all the employees? Why do so many people want to work here?

A: I think it's about encouraging people to be good at what they do and do what they're good at. Also, giving them a lot of freedom to be able to be creative. And then, you know, sort of trying to get out of the way.

Q: How big of a role would you say fate has played in the growth of Columbia Sportswear?

A: I think there's some luck involved in the success of a business. Who knows what percentage it is? I think luck has more to do with the timing, because if you're doing the right things, you're going to stumble on those things that are good with more frequency.

Q: Humor plays a very involved role in your marketing and in your corporate culture. Has that been a principle that you've adhered to?

A: Yes, the sense of humor thing. People can take business way too seriously. I am in favor of having a good time when you're working hard. Life's too short. We're talking about apparel products; we're not talking about cures for diseases.

Q: You like to take things lightly, but do you feel there's a greater purpose behind what you've been doing?

A: Certainly if you start looking at how many people are employed by the company and the responsibility that you have to make sure that the wheels keep going around. That's significant. There's also a certain reliance on the company for being a benefactor to needy groups globally.

Q: Running a large company, I'm sure you encounter adversity on a daily basis. How are you able to overcome adversity time and time again?

A: There can be adverse problems or issues that come up. The key is, we know we have to get through it, so how do you break it down into bite-sized chunks that you can attack and solve. I think that's the way it has to be done. We try to attack these issues. They're going to come up every day, you better be able to handle it. Otherwise, you're really going to be constrained as to how big you can get.

Q: On the lighter side, how has it been working side-by-side with your mother for so many years? A lot of people would say, "Oh, I could never work with my parents."

A: Well, they'd be right. [Laughing] Certainly there are tensions and issues that are just between parents and their children that don't exist between others. Early on, we were able to do a good job segregating the various duties that we had. Then those issues tended to have less impact on the business.

Q: Would you say that the entrepreneurial spirit was in your blood?

A: Maybe. My grandfather brought his family here. He was probably my age when they immigrated from Germany. I often look back and say, he basically gave up everything he had to drag his family over to Portland. He was probably a pretty big risk-taker.

Q: Who were the people that made the greatest impression on you during your childhood?

A: My childhood, I don't remember back that far. [Laughing] I'll think about that one and get back to you. Certainly, my parents and my grandparents, but I'm sure there's somebody else.

Q: What kind of education did you have?

A: I went to parochial grade school. Then I went to an all-boys Jesuit high school.

Q: Was that tough, the Jesuit education?

A: Well, yes. I was a miserable student

Q: Is that because you were just goofing off?

A: Either that or I was stupid, one of the two. [Laughing] Probably because I was stupid. [Laughing]

Q: I don't think so.

A: [Laughing] But then when I got to college at the University of Oregon, I was amazed at how easy it was. Now, that doesn't mean that I got good grades in college because it was easy. It just means that I thought about what I had to do to get a C and then I did two percent less than that.

Q: So you were able to survive on C's in college?

A: Oh yes. I didn't see any reason to get more than a C. I just wanted to pass.

Q: Did you have a good time?

A: I had a great time. [Laughing]

Q: Was it your father's passing away that made the transition for you? Is that what made you more serious?

A: Yes, probably, because the business had been so intertwined in the family. It was not in great shape. It was basically going to be on me. My mom had not been in the business before.

Q: So you took on the responsibility and went into the family business. Family means a lot to you doesn't it?

A: Yes.

Q: Talking about family, how long have you been married for?

A: One hundred and nine years. [Laughing] I think this coming year it should be thirty-three years.

Q: I just got married two years ago, I'm striving for that. What would you advise?

A: It gets worse. [Laughing] You'll soon find out how miserable it could get. [Laughing]

Q: Seriously, how has your wife helped you over the years?

A: She has been very supportive.

Q: Is she your boss?

A: Yes.

Q: Trying to make up for what you said about it getting worse?

A: Yes. [Laughing]

Q: How many kids do you have?

A: I have two kids. I have a twenty-two year old that just graduated from the University of Washington.

Q: Congratulations.

A: Thanks.

Q: C's or better?

A: Actually he did better. All our kids have done really well.

Q: Genetically speaking, generations tend to improve.

A: It would be hard to do worse. [Laughing]

Q: You work with your mother and you seem to have a very successful family. What has family meant to you throughout your life?

A: I think the important thing is to try to be moderate in the stuff that you do so that you make sure to include the family in everything you can. It's a balancing act.

Q: How do you balance it?

A: Well, something has to give unfortunately. My wife would say the family has given more than the business. I mean, if you get up at four in the morning so that you can do your e-mails, it's tough.

Q: You and your family have accumulated quite a bit of wealth. How has that changed your life?

A: Not very much really. I probably still work as much as I ever did. You know, I enjoy what I do so I'm here a lot and when I'm not here, I'm working. I was invited to a Merrill Lynch conference. I told them I'm not doing this for the money and everybody laughed at me. [Laughing]

Q: Investment bankers will definitely laugh at that. Outside of work, how have you most enjoyed spending your time?

A: I used to do a lot of fly-fishing for trout and salmon, and quite a bit of bird hunting—some years I'll be able to go four or five days a week. I also play golf in the summertime, maybe three times a week.

Q: So that's why you're up at four o'clock in the morning?

A: I have to! [Laughing]

Q: When you have a bad day, what do you do to rejuvenate your spirits?

A: Well, it's never horrible. We've certainly had our problems, but you have to do what you can do about it and after that there's not much you can do.

Q: You seem to take life in stride.

A: You have to be pragmatic. You have to spend time on the stuff that's important.

Q: Over the course of your life, what have you learned from experience and from making mistakes?

A: I guess the number one thing is that you better be a very good listener and be willing to accept criticism.

Q: Do you have any regrets?

A: I wish I was taller and thinner. [Laughing]

Q: What does your wife have to say about that?

A: She would agree. [Laughing]

Q: Joking aside, would you say you're one to follow your heart or your mind?

A: Hopefully, my mind. I try to be reasonably pragmatic.

Q: Do you also follow your passion?

A: Yes, sometimes a course of action will appear to be very clear to me (when it's) not necessarily clear to everybody else.

Q: Does it come to you in the form of an understanding or a vision?

A: A lightning bolt. [Laughing] Well, you know, somebody once told me that, "After two drinks I can run any business." [Laughing] I'm not sure I can run any business, but certain underlying precepts run throughout almost all businesses in my opinion. It seems pretty clear to me what they are. They're generally very simple. Some people get in trouble because they want to make things way too complicated.

Q: What would you say is the secret of staying passionate over the years, not just in business but in life?

A: You've got to like what you do. I mean really. If you enjoy what you do, I can't imagine not being excited about going and doing it. It's more than just work, it's the kind of stuff that you do when you're not working too. It better be fun.

Q: Do you think that people tend to make too many decisions based on money?

A: Yes, it's probably too big a motivator. At the end of the day, if people did what they liked, they probably would end up being happier. It might cost you today, but in the future you'll be rewarded and you'll be happier.

Q: How crucial is it to keep hope and be an optimist?

A: I think it's critical. Your fate is in your own hands. If you're not optimistic about your opportunities, you really should be changing something. You've got nobody to blame but yourself.

Q: You said earlier you feel a responsibility to your employees. What principles are involved in being a good leader?

A: Willingness to take risk, and confidence in your abilities to define the right path.

Q: How about inspiring other people?

A: I think it's great to get training in sales, because it's important whether you're selling photocopy machines or you're trying to convince your team that they are on the right path. It's all about selling and communication skills and making sure that people understand your position and why it's the right position.

Q: On a broader scale, what role has society played in your life?

A: It has provided a great market for our products. [Laughing] Society is always right. [Laughing]

Q: Are there any other aspects about society that fill you with hope?

A: People are much more informed than they ever were—I think in general for the good.

Q: Do you think our society as a whole needs a more defined purpose?

A: I would say the education of people in the world today. Education is a good thing; it makes you realize how close you are. I mean, there isn't much difference between people really. I think the similarities are much more overriding than the differences.

Q: If you had the power to change one thing about the world, what would it be?

A: Tolerance has improved, but it's not anywhere as good as it needs to get. If you could only make people better listeners, more tolerant, less likely to blame somebody else.

Q: So after everything is said and done, what do you find most important in life?

A: I think it's most important that you're a good human being, that you made a contribution and made a difference.

Timothy's skills as a corporate leader are a product of his ability to take risks, make decisions, and have the vision to see what others cannot. He's also a strong communicator, with the talent to empower and motivate his team. But despite these remarkable qualities, it is his ability to find fulfillment in life that is most outstanding. No matter what the situation, he remains cheerful, positive and good-humored. Timothy truly cherishes life.

Talking with one of the richest people in America caused me to reflect on the meaning of wealth. So often in life, we don't appreciate what we have, because we're always trying to get something more. A religious leader once told me, "A wealthy man is not one who has the most. A wealthy man most appreciates what he has." Depending on his state of mind, a rich man can feel poor or a poor man can feel rich. Timothy feels good about who he is as a person, enjoys what he does for living, loves his family, and manages to have fun on top of it all. What makes Timothy truly rich is not his money, but his appreciation for what he has.

Many of us constantly search for happiness in our lives, without appreciating what we already have. The grass is rarely greener on the other side. It's merely an illusion. Once you get there you will realize you are still the same person. If you weren't happy before, chances are, you won't be happy now. The answers to finding fulfillment in life are not to be found in the outside world, in anything or anyone. The answers are inside each of us. Appreciate what you have, and you will find true wealth and fulfillment.

—Chapter 11—

Work Ethic

Baruch Blumberg, M.D., Ph.D.

Are there any short cuts in life? Is hard work the only way to get to where you want to be?

Baruch Blumberg is best known for his work with the Hepatitis-B Virus. Not only did he discover the virus that causes this disease, but he also developed a way to diagnose it in patients, and went on to invent the vaccine. As a result of his work, countless lives have been saved. For his lasting impact on society, Baruch won the Nobel Prize in Medicine in 1976, and continues to be recognized as one of the greatest living scientists in the world.

Much of his life's work, nearly four decades, has been dedicated to the research of Hepatitis and other infectious diseases at the Fox Chase Cancer Center in Philadelphia. Baruch has also worked on disease prevention at the National Institutes of Health. Several years ago, he served as the Director of the NASA Astrobiology Institute.

Baruch, who holds a M.D. from Columbia University and a Ph.D. from Oxford University, decided to focus his career on medical research in order to help the greatest number of people. Although most of his time has been spent as a researcher, Baruch has also enjoyed interaction with students as a professor of both medicine and anthropology at the University of Pennsylvania. Adding to his distinguished resume, he has also taught and served as a visiting professor at Stanford University, the Indian Institute of Science in Bangalore, and the University of Otago in New Zealand.

Baruch has been married for many years to his wife Jean, who is an artist. They have four children, all of whom are grown and have families of their own. Baruch is extremely proud of his children and grandchildren and feels that family has been the most important part of his life, and the source of motivation behind his success.

I met Baruch at his brownstone in the historic district of Philadelphia, Pennsylvania:

Q: In the early days of your research, did you conceive that your work could have such great impact on the world?

A: I always had this idea that if I worked hard, what I did would have an impact. I didn't know in what way.

Q: How does it make you feel knowing that your research has saved millions of lives and impacted society in such a great way?

A: It's a wonderful feeling. It has exceeded my wildest expectations.

Q: What was the thought process that led to your idea?

A: There was a series of events. Discovery is a process, even though it's often dramatized as a single "brainstorm".

Q: Are you as passionate today about your work as you were when you first started?

A: I'm not sure the term "passionate" is appropriate. I am as excited and interested now as I was then, but passion usually means an abandonment of reason.

Q: A scientist can't have that happen to him?

A: Well, you have to be careful about it. You can be enthusiastic, but you also have to maintain objectivity. You don't want to go overboard. That's easy to do.

Q: What does it take to be an inventor or revolutionary thinker?

A: You have to be open to new ideas. You can't go into everything with a fixed notion about what you're going to find. You have to know that you're supposed to discover new stuff. It's odd, scientific training very often doesn't give you that insight that you're supposed to find new things.

Q: You have to deviate from the normal path?

A: Yes.

Q: Has work made you happy?

A: Oh yes, it has. I've had nice people to work with, a fascinating, interesting bunch.

Q: You seem like you've been very positive throughout your life.

A: I think scientists in general tend to be optimistic, because if you don't think that you can solve the problem then there's no way it can be solved. And then my generation is very optimistic. Our generation has been called the *Lucky Generation*. We went through difficult times—World War II, the Depression and all that. But generally speaking, my generation was very optimistic.

Q: Do difficult times teach you how to overcome adversity in the future?

A: Nietzsche said that what does not destroy you only makes you stronger.

Q: But how do you prevent yourself from becoming cynical?

A: By recognizing that the world is ironic. That it is often the opposite of what you think it should be. Once you recognize that, then everything fits into place. [Laughing]

Q: What do you believe is the reason that you've become so successful?

A: One reason is luck. The other reason is I've worked at good places and institutions that have provided the right atmosphere.

Q: Are there specific life principles that guide you?

A: Yes, hard work. If you want to achieve, you must really work hard, and I mean long, long hours.

Q: Work is obviously important, but let's get more philosophical. What do you believe is the meaning of life?

A: Do you know the story about the old rabbi who is dying and all the students gather around him? His oldest student, who is a distinguished scholar in his own right, is standing by his bedside, and right next to him is the next senior student, a very distinguished scholar as well. So it goes right down the line, which is filled with his many students, all the way to the youngest. The oldest disciple whispers, "Rabbi, what is life? Rabbi, what is life?" The Rabbi sort of takes it in and thinks about it, and then with what appears to be his last breath he says, in a feeble voice, "Life is a river." So the students say, "Oh my God, life is a river, life is a river!" And it's passed right down to the last student. But the last student, who is the youngest and most curious, hears that and says,

"Why is life a river?" So the question is relayed all the way back up the line and when the most senior student hears this question, he turns to the Rabbi and says, "Rabbi, why is life a river?" The Rabbi again pulls himself together, thinks about it, and says, "So it's not a river." Does that answer your question? [Laughing] I mean it's one of these unanswerable questions. It's a lot of things. It may be a river; it may be something else. [Laughing]

Q: So the meaning of life is elusive, but can we at least find meaning in ourselves? How essential is self-awareness?

A: My thinking gets a bit compulsive. I keep a chronological record and diary of what I've done. That leads to self-awareness and gives you a sense of direction. I'm always expecting that something unexpected will happen, and, in a sense, I am waiting for it. So the thing to do is to know when opportunity arises and then follow it. Was it Yogi Berra who said, "When you come to a fork in the road, pick it up"? [Laughing]

Q: Faced with so many choices in life, how do you choose what's right for you?

A: I remember my early career, when I had a variety of job offers. One of my criteria was that I took the one that paid least. I like the idea of having money and being comfortable, but I don't want to work exclusively for money. I think a lot of scientists are that way. They much prefer to do something interesting than make a few extra bucks.

Q: Are you one to follow your heart or your mind or a combination?

A: One of the problems with science is that people think that you can use rational scientific reason exclusively to solve problems. It's not true for all problems.

Q: Is it more important to be flexible so that you can adjust to changes in life, or steadfast so that you can weather the storm?

A: You want both. Steadfastness is *numero uno*, but the ability to change is crucial.

Q: So how should you approach life?

A: Work hard. Be serious about life. You have a responsibility to do something. It's a great sin to waste your life.

Q: What is the secret to having a happy, fulfilled and successful life?

A: Well, in a way being always somewhat dissatisfied. If you're satisfied, you're not going anywhere. Actually, I see the attraction of being more relaxed, and sometimes I wish I could be like that more. I know my wife wishes I could be like that more. But I think this notion of being dissatisfied is important. I mean, there have been times when I thought everything was going okay and things were content and I still felt dissatisfied. [Laughing]

Q: Dissatisfaction may lead to success in your life, but does it also lead to happiness and fulfillment?

A: It's kind of a paradox. [Laughing]

Q: Do you work so hard because you feel a greater sense of responsibility to society?

A: I would say I've always sort of felt that. One of the reasons I went into medicine is that you can do a lot of good very easily. If you get people better, that's a wonderful thing.

Q: You have a wife Jean and four children. Would your successes be as meaningful without your family?

A: In many ways you seek achievements to gain the approval of your children. They tend to keep you humble. [Laughing]

Q: What has given you the greatest satisfaction in your life?

A: My grandchildren and children are a great source of joy. You know, it's up and down sometimes, but they're very good kids. And of course the recognition by my colleagues is important. The fact that my work resulted in saving many lives is enormously gratifying.

Q: After everything is said and done, how do you want to be remembered?

A: Being part of a family—and that I prevented misery and sickness for many people.

Baruch Blumberg has been able to accomplish just about everything imaginable in his life. While in the navy, he was a commanding officer of a landing ship. After his military service, he went on to attain an M.D. and Ph.D. at some of the most prestigious schools in the world. As a doctor, he helped the sick by working at hospitals and traveling on relief missions to Third World countries. He has worked as a professor at some of the most elite universities in the world, and his medical discoveries have positively impacted millions of lives, and resulted in a Nobel Prize. Baruch demonstrates the value of a strong work ethic, built upon focus, commitment and a long-term perspective. He does not fathom being lazy or failing to do his absolute best at everything he does. For Baruch, wasting one's potential in life is a great sin.

While Baruch believes in hard work, he understands that work must be constantly balanced with other things we enjoy, such as family, friends, hobbies and interests. Besides having a loving wife, and many wonderful children and grandchildren, Baruch has been an avid outdoorsman who has made time for daily activities such as rowing, running and other physical exercise. This balance leads to a full, meaningful life, keeping him happy, passionate and refreshed.

For Baruch Blumberg, there are no short cuts in life. He believes that if you keep working and doing your best each day, over time there's a good chance you will get everything that life has to offer. Work hard, be patient, manage to have fun in the process, and you will be well on your way to true success. Promotion, achievement, study, experience, reflection, religion, travel, sport, friendship, family, love, romance—you will get everything that you want out of life, if you're willing to work for it!

—CHAPTER 12—

FAITH

RAYMOND DAMADIAN, M.D.

Does God exist? Which religion is right? How does faith help us in our lives?

Raymond Damadian is the inventor of the MRI, a device that has revolutionized medicine with its ability to scan the human body. In addition to its other uses, MRI technology has transformed the way cancer and other diseases are detected, leading to earlier, more effective treatment, and potentially saving lives. For his groundbreaking work, Raymond has been awarded the National Medal of Technology by the President of the United States and inducted into the National Inventors Hall of Fame. Raymond has an M.D. from Albert Einstein College of Medicine at Yeshiva University.

In 1978, Raymond founded Fonar Corporation to market his patented MRI technology. With its patent protection, Fonar seemed to be destined to take over a multi-billion dollar emerging market. However, large companies such as GE, Hitachi, Toshiba and Siemens ignored the patent rights and jumped into the market.

Although Fonar was a small company with limited resources, Raymond was determined to protect his rights in court. After a long and frustrating battle, justice finally prevailed in 1997, when the United States Supreme Court ordered GE to pay Fonar a $128.7 million settlement for its patent infringement. Today, Raymond is still the Chairman and President of Fonar, a NASDAQ traded company located in Melville, New York.

Raymond has been happily married to his wife, Donna, for over forty years. They met while Raymond was still in medical school, working as a tennis professional on Long Island during the summer. Donna and Raymond have successfully raised three children together, and place a strong emphasis on family life. A man of profound faith and stern Christian principle, Raymond strongly believes in Biblical values, divine guidance and a strict interpretation of religious law. By conducting his personal and business life accordingly, he strives to win God's grace. Raymond is very critical of society, particularly its loose morals and corrupt institutions. He is a man who especially detests dishonesty and deception.

I met with Raymond at Fonar's national headquarters in Melville, New York:

Q: You are the inventor of the MRI, winner of the National Medal of Technology, and an inductee into the National Inventors Hall of Fame—would you have ever conceived that you would be where you're at today?

A: It's a great honor to have been acknowledged in one's lifetime for an important contribution to mankind.

Q: How does it make you feel knowing that your invention has saved many, many lives?

A: I went into medicine in the first place, because I wanted to be able to contribute my labors to helping people. That's why I chose medicine.

Q: Have you striven for a greater purpose?

A: I think that the right purpose in life, and it has taken me a long time to understand this, is to dedicate your life to glorifying the Almighty.

Q: What do you think are the most important life principles that have made you so successful?

A: I think the most important thing to understand is that the goal is not to be successful in business; the goal is to do what's right. I think people that miss this understanding often mistakenly set their goals to amass wealth. When the emptiness of such an objective is eventually discovered, the disappointment can be profound. Too often, the biography of the wealth seeker ends up reading like a Greek tragedy. I believe that it's innate in everybody to want to be able to truthfully say to themselves that, "While I passed this way, I did something fruitful." It's more than sufficient, in my view, to be able to point to the fact that I invested myself in my wife and my children. I think it is more than enough to feel that you have done the best you can in the gainful service of the Lord.

Q: You have such a profound way of looking at things. It makes me want to know more about your life history. Growing up, what kind of family situation did you have?

A: Excellent—wonderful, devoted parents. My father was an immigrant who had gone through the Armenian Holocaust at the hands of the Turks. Almost two million people died in that genocide during the First World War for their Christian beliefs.

Q: Did your father's background make you think about issues from his past?

A: A little bit, but not much, because he was a wonderful gentleman whose entire existence was invested in his children.

Q: Did you have any other role models growing up?

A: Just people that you saw from a distance. The years that I spent competing in athletics were very formative. In sports, you have to take risks. Playing it safe is rarely adequate. There were people in the athletic arena that I admired both for their skill and their character.

Q: What were your goals when you first started off, early on in your life?

A: I would say I was like most undergraduates, not too sure what I wanted to do. Medicine was a good career choice because its scope was very broad, and it left open the greatest number of options. You could be a missionary, a scientist, an administrator of a hospital, or a family physician.

Q: That's the advantage of having a good education also.

A: It leaves a lot of doors open.

Q: What has family meant to you in your life?

A: Well, I think it was ordained to be the centerpiece of every person's existence, and those who trifle with it end up suffering mightily.

Q: You've been married how long now?

A: Forty-four years.

Q: So what do you think is the secret to having a strong family over the years?

A: That's a very profound question because of what's going on in society. The threats to family integrity are spiraling upwards. What would have been threats ten years ago are harsh realities today. There is really only one answer, and it is what's advised in the Old Testament—there will be only a remnant that is preserved, and that remnant is the remnant that trusts the Lord. I think to answer your question in a specific way, read the Bible everyday. My wife and I pray together and we ask for protection from the Almighty. We do that regularly. It works.

Q: You've been a devoted husband and father for over four decades, as well as a renowned inventor. What is most important to you in your life?

A: The Lord, my wife and my family. When you're young and ambitious, you tend to put more focus on career and what you're doing. As you get older, you get wiser, and realize that it's a false chase.

Q: What role has faith played in your life?

A: It's about getting to the point where you can trust in the Lord. In my own life, it has been rare when my prayers have gone unanswered. Some merely have been delayed. A few have been rejected, and I later was grateful they weren't answered. Paul teaches in Romans 8:28 that "All things work together for good to them that love God, to them who are called according to his purpose." We went into a patent battle with the mighty General Electric. There wasn't anybody out there that gave us the slightest prospect of prevailing against what many say is the world's most powerful company. We did.

Q: Do you think business ethics today are not what they should be?

A: It's interesting that you should touch on it. That's another thing that I find fascinating. People who are less than honorable in their business dealings always puzzle me. It's puzzling because only a fraction of understanding would make it obvious that the greatest currency a businessperson can have is the ability to be trusted.

Q: It's also just about being a good human being.

A: Yes, striving to that end. I'll tell you something else that's interesting. Take a community like Wall Street, as an example. The Bible teaches that the love of money is the root of all evil; it doesn't teach that money itself is evil. I feel sad for the people of Wall Street, because what drives so many of them is literally the love of money.

Q: Our society is saturated with successful people who lack ethics. How do you reconcile that?

A: I think the best way to address that is by questioning what's meant by success. What is the definition of success? Success is in the eye of the beholder. I think the proper definition of success, if one is even needed, is whether or not you're seeking favor with the Lord.

Q: What does integrity actually mean to you?

A: I think it means honesty in all aspects of your endeavors. I once heard a definition of truth that I liked—"Free of the intent to deceive." It's a very demanding definition, but it's also profound. I try to live by it.

Q: Do you think that values change over time, and if so, how have society's values changed during the course of your lifetime?

A: I think that the most destructive development has been the breakdown of sexual mores. The destructiveness of it is ghastly—divorce, infidelity. Once sexual mores are broken, once the fundamental integrity of relationships has broken, everything else fails as a consequence. I think a nation is a simple composite of its building blocks. The foundation that every society is built upon is the family. So once the integrity of the family has been breeched, a failing nation cannot be far behind. History, as well as the Bible, teaches that again and again.

Q: As a result of technology, have we grown more or less connected to one another as people?

A: That's a tough question. I think probably the best answer is less connected. I think the reason I would argue less connected is the multiplicity of facilities that technology has created. The overall result is the limitless range of distractions mankind now has from its ordained purpose to serve the Lord.

Q: Do you think our society needs a greater, more defined purpose?

A: I don't know that you need to define it for society itself. I think it really needs to get defined for the individual, and society will follow.

Q: Along what lines should the individual have purpose?

A: To invest their lives to serve the Lord with their gifts and labors.

Q: If you had the power to change one thing, what would that be?

A: That's easy. I would stop Hollywood and the media from generating their obscenities. I think it's by far the most destructive element in our society. It's always defended by the First Amendment, (but) it's obviously not what was intended by the writers of the First Amendment. It was never their legislative intent for "free speech" to be perverted into a vehicle for selling obscenity and degrading humanity.

Q: You have such purpose and passion in all your beliefs. What's the secret to staying passionate over the years?

A: You are really asking a fundamental question. Where does one get his inspiration? If you have God's Word as an integral part of your life, you will be in the Holy Spirit, from whom you will get inspiration. I think that's why it's true that modern science and the modern scientific era in which we live, spearheaded by Da Vinci,

Galileo and Copernicus in the 1500's and passing on to Newton, Faraday and Pasteur, arose after the printing of Gutenberg's Bible and not before. All were devout, and it is clear from their writings that access to God's Word in print supplied the inspiration that gave us the modern scientific era. While remarkably little happened between 350 BC and 1455 AD, once Gutenberg's Bible was released in 1455, the world exploded into the modern scientific era. Isaac Newton once said, "If from reading my work, the people who read it are guided to the pursuit of coming to know and trusting the Almighty—nothing from use of my work would give me greater pleasure."

Q: After everything is said and done, how would you want to be remembered?

A: I don't know. I don't think it's important. I think it really comes down to, what is it going to be when I face my Maker?

Q: Do you want to be remembered as a good person?

A: Of course. I'd like to be remembered as honorable and trustworthy, and as a good father. (Those are) the things that count, that are important.

After a lifetime of study, Raymond is convinced that God's presence is irrefutable, therefore his ultimate purpose in life is to glorify, serve, and find favor with the Almighty. Raymond believes that God gives us strength in overcoming adversity, offers guidance in finding the right direction, and instills essential qualities such as humility, empathy, integrity, commitment and leadership. Raymond urges other people to pray, read the Bible, ask for direction, and trust in the Lord, because he feels that this is the surest path to a happy and fruitful life.

A skeptic might ask, *does God really exist or is He just a figment of our imagination created to make us feel better about our lives*? The answer is simple—everyone has to look inside their heart and find their own sense of faith. But whatever you choose to believe, there is no denying that for Raymond Damadian and many others, faith has brought purpose, conviction and wisdom. Faith has helped to maintain family life and has inspired many people to be better, more caring human beings. Faith has offered hope of a safer world and a better tomorrow. Without faith, life would be very difficult to endure.

But what of the conflicts religion has created throughout history and in the world today? Christianity, Judaism, Muslimism, Buddhism, Hinduism, which one is right? In this context, we spend too much time worrying about right and wrong. At the core of all the great religions in the world, are the same fundamental lessons—worship God, follow a righteous life, love your neighbor, maintain peace, practice humility, show gratitude, and achieve wisdom. If we would just follow these common principles, we would forget our differences and together solve many problems in the world.

—CHAPTER 13—

SELF-AWARENESS

ELLEN GORDON

Who are you? What do you want in life? What are you meant to do? What direction should you choose?

For the last three decades, Ellen Gordon has been president of the Tootsie Roll Company, working closely with her husband Melvin, who is chairman. Together they own approximately thirty-seven percent of the company. It is the third largest candy manufacturer in the country with such brands as Tootsie Rolls, Charms, Blow-Pops, Junior Mints, Charleston Chew, Sugar Daddies and Andes. In 1978, Ellen became only the second woman in history to be a president of a company traded on the New York Stock Exchange. Although her accomplishments made her one of the early trailblazers for women's rights, she has not necessarily identified herself with the feminist movement. Throughout her career, she has simply been doing what she adores, and getting a chance to work side by side with her loving husband. If she has become a women's rights leader in the process, then that's fine by her.

Now in her seventies, Ellen continues to work out of pleasure rather than financial necessity. Ellen has never had to work; she grew up in an extremely privileged family. Blessed with financial security, she could have been staying at home, participating in the local social events and even playing tennis at the country club. But Ellen has always treasured qualities such as a strong work ethic, discipline and commitment. To this day, she works countless hours every week, including most weekends.

Ellen met Melvin Gordon when they were both vacationing in Florida. After a romantic courtship, they married on June 25, 1950. In the early years of her marriage, family was Ellen's main priority. She didn't work and even left school to be a good wife and mother. But over time, she realized that she could combine her domestic life with her other dreams, and decided to go back to school in order to receive her bachelors degree from Brandeis University. Having achieved her academic goals, Ellen decided to work at Tootsie Roll. As she learned the ropes, she took on more and more responsibility. In time, Ellen realized that she not only loved to work, but she truly excelled in a business environment. She and her husband have helped make Tootsie Roll more successful than ever before.

Ellen and Melvin Gordon take pride in having a very close, strong family. Their four daughters, raised with a familiar conservative value system, turned out humble, grounded and hard-working. Ellen and Melvin are happy grandparents, and although their children's families live all over the country, they make a point of gathering together several times a year. Through Tootsie Roll and other personal contributions, the Gordon family has made charity an extremely important part of their lives. Their biggest social causes have been fighting poverty, improving education and funding medical research. As company owners, they also feel a great deal of responsibility for Tootsie Roll and all of the people associated with it.

I met with Ellen at Tootsie Roll national headquarters in Chicago, Illinois:

Q: What does it take to run an enormous company like Tootsie Roll?

A: It takes a wonderful organization, and it takes a lot of energy to run such a company. It also takes a lot of hard work and thinking about what needs to be done, now and in the future.

Q: You were the second woman in the history of the New York Stock Exchange to be a president of a company. Was it difficult for you to break through the gender barriers at the time? Did you feel any kind of societal pressures working against you?

A: Well, there were just some odd things. I went to the New York Stock Exchange. They said, "We've never had a woman up on this floor before." There weren't many women in business at the time.

Q: But you didn't let that stop you?

A: You just have to go on. Today, it isn't so unusual. There are many women executives and heads of companies. It's very exciting!

Q: What were your original goals and intentions for your career?

A: Everything just sort of happened. When I was graduating from high school, I was sixteen, and the teachers said, "Write about what you're going to do when you grow up." I wrote a paper about how I really wanted to be a businesswoman, but then I ended the paper by saying, "But I also want to get married and have a lot of kids." It was expected of me.

Q: How old were you when you got married?

A: Eighteen. Although I had school and work in the back of my mind, I didn't dream it would become a reality. In between my third and fourth child, I went back to school, and then to graduate school. I had an opportunity to take a course for women executives.

I took it and found out that I was fascinated by it. Only after that did I start to work, and I found that I loved it.

Q: Why do you love work so much?

A: First of all, we have fun products and it's something I can relate to very easily. But also, there are a lot of challenges. I like the puzzle, and I like the solving.

Q: How difficult is it for a woman to balance work with family?

A: Very difficult. There may be certain times in your life you work harder, and there are other times you have more of a family obligation. You can have it all, but maybe not all at the same time. It is possible, but there are give-ups. There's no doubt about it.

Q: You've been working with your husband for many years. How does that work?

A: Well, it presents an interesting challenge. We've done it for a lot of years. We're used to it.

Q: Is it nice because you get a chance to spend a lot of time with one another?

A: We spend a lot of time together, and you have to decide how you're going to do it. Every couple that works together does it differently. But it has worked very well for us for a long time, and we kind of complement each other. We work problems out together. Then you take him home with you on the weekends, and that's nice too.

Q: What are the greatest adversities you've had to overcome over the years?

A: You know, I never thought about adversities. You sort of think, "Well, this issue came up, and it has to be dealt with." There are always problems.

Q: So how are you able to recover so well from problems and failures?

A: It's not easy. It shakes your confidence sometimes. You have to make sure that your path makes sense. What helps is that we do a lot of work in teams here. We advise each other and work together.

Q: When you have a bad day full of problems and failures, what do you do to rejuvenate your spirits?

A: Try to talk it out. Try to think it out. And I'm a big believer in sleep. When you have to make a decision, and you're having a bad time, sleep on it, and it makes a little more sense. I do believe that sleep refreshes; I feel very strongly about that.

Q: Looking back, do you have any regrets about life or work?

A: No, no.

Q: Everything is very positive?

A: Once in a while I say, "Well, if I thought about it, maybe I would have this." But there's no point. You have to move on. If you make a mistake, you have to correct it.

Q: Growing up in a rather well-to-do family, you never had to feel any pressure to support yourself. Why did you become so grounded and hard-working?

A: My family was very conservative. They were very frugal. They did not believe in wasting money. They didn't believe in display or show.

Q: What kind of impact did education have on your life?

A: It had a lot. The world of books—just a lot.

Q: So was it instrumental in building your foundation and confidence?

A: Absolutely, yes. The confidence always increases. As time goes on, you feel a little better about things. You gather just another block of what you understand in this enormous puzzle of the world, and that's exciting. That's what education does.

Q: Do you think education also teaches you to understand other people?

A: Absolutely. The other thing that I felt that really taught me to understand other people was watching children grow up. Amazing how much you learn watching children when they're young, before all the inhibitions.

Q: In so many facets of life—having children, attaining an education and building a business—you've been so successful. What kind of life principles have helped you become successful in work and in life?

A: Obviously, you have to be very straightforward and honest, so character. Also, be persistent. I think that's one of the most important things. Melvin's football coach told him, "Don't trip over the first blade of grass." You have to be determined. "If you're blocked, you go around it, or you go under it, or you go over it." If you can't do that, you just won't do it. And you learn to develop the people. It's important to develop the people around you, because you can't do it all yourself.

Q: How would you advise other people to make it happen in their lives?

A: Work hard, and work smart hard.

Q: What does that mean?

A: You have to really think it through and think through all the ramifications. I think it's important to do that. Don't jeopardize the future for immediate bottom-line gains.

Q: Does part of your success stem from a pressure that you feel, whether it's from society or from yourself, to achieve great things?

A: Oh yes, (to) keep going on. I don't know about great things, but you have to achieve. You have to do right. You have to do better.

Q: As a business leader, what do you think about all the unscrupulous people in society that become successful, prominent figures, even though they lack integrity? How do you reconcile that?

A: You can't reconcile that. There's no leeway. Zero tolerance. You have to have integrity. You have to do things right. You have to surround yourself with people who have that belief.

Q: Do you consider yourself a steward?

A: Yes, you are a steward. And you are a servant. You really need to serve other people. I've always felt that. As businesspeople, we're all servants, to serve our various constituencies—from shareholders, to employees, to suppliers, to customers.

Q: So you believe that, as a leader, you have a responsibility to act in a more ethical way, in order to be a role model for society?

A: Absolutely. The higher your position of leadership, the more responsibility you have (and) the less leeway. People are looking up to you. You have to be very vigilant.

Q: Is that why it has been so important for you to be involved in charity work?

A: I think it's important to give back to society. It's important to be connected, to give back when you're in a privileged situation.

Q: As someone who cares about the well-being of society, what aspects about society fill you with the greatest hope?

A: Human beings have this resilience, determination.

Q: On the other hand, what are the biggest problems in society?

A: If you could only make people be kinder to each other and less cynical.

Q: If you had the power to change one thing in the world, what would it be?

A: Feed the people, keep them healthy, make sure that they have fresh water, fresh food. Keep them free of disease and give them a chance in the basic things that make them happy. But you can't just give it to them, because I don't think people can maintain it, if it's given to them. They have to participate.

Q: To finish the interview on a more philosophical note, what's the secret to being happy and fulfilled in life?

A: Doing what you like, and what you find challenging. If everything is fairly smooth—people have their health and avoid any huge calamities—then there's a good chance (for happiness).

Q: What do you believe is the meaning of life?

A: You have to stop along the way and enjoy the process. See where it takes you, the road; it's so varied. It's very interesting to see how you adapt and what you do. You have to feel the way.

Q: So you have to have a good sense of self-awareness?

A: I think you have to constantly examine yourself and analyze yourself and what you like. You have to think about what your effect is on people. You need to think—do I want this? Do I want that? Why don't I want that? What has brought me to that?

Q: Is it a matter of being honest with yourself about everything? Is that something you think about?

A: You know, yes I do. Sometimes I come to an opinion, and I say, "Come on Ellen, now what's the real reason." So kind of peel that onion down a little more and find out what's the core, what's inside.

Q: Throughout your life, what have you had the greatest love for?

A: Family, my work. I think those two things. You feel really good when you do something for somebody.

During my meeting with Ellen Gordon, I was most impressed by her strong sense of self-awareness. Ellen is introspective about the constant complexities, contradictions and choices of life. Ellen continually asks herself questions about what she wants, who she is, how she got here and where she is going. Taking the time to think about many of these questions, Ellen is able to find the right direction.

A large part of self-awareness is being honest with yourself about your thoughts, hopes and decisions in life. It was this quality in Ellen that prevented her from relinquishing her pursuits of education and business. After being a housewife and mother for a number of years, Ellen wanted a chance to pursue her other dreams. Her honest self-reflection, combined with her intelligence and her ability to act, allowed her to try new things, improve herself, and eventually end up in the position she is today.

In life, there are many unknowns and many difficult choices. It's hard at times to find our way and understand how we fit into the world. *Who am I? What do I want? Where am I going in life? What am I meant to do?* We can never stop asking ourselves these questions. If we don't pause at times along the way to assess our lives, time passes like a blur, without meaning or comprehension. In a way, by asking ourselves these questions, we mark our existence. We can say, *Yes, I am here, and this is who I am.* In so doing, we remind ourselves of our dreams and desires, and eventually get closer to the truth.

—CHAPTER 14—

HONESTY

RUSSELL HULSE, PH.D.

Are there truly honest people in this world? What's the advantage of being honest?

Russell Hulse is a world-renowned physicist who currently works at the Princeton University Plasma Physics Laboratory. In 1993, Russell was awarded the Nobel Prize in Physics for the discovery of a binary pulsar. A pulsar is a rapidly rotating neutron star, the collapsed remnant left over from a supernova explosion. As opposed to most pulsars that exist as solitary objects, binary pulsars travel in unison. Through long years of careful measurement and analysis, the study of the binary pulsar has supplied some of the best real-world evidence confirming Einstein's Theory of Relativity and Gravitation.

Russell holds a Ph.D. in Physics from the University of Massachusetts, but he is not one to be defined by prestigious awards and fancy degrees. At his core, Russell loves science—the curiosity, the discovery, and the quest for knowledge. For this man, science is a profound and even spiritual experience. What impressed me most about Russell is that while he has accomplished much in a difficult field, he remains warm, sincere, and open. He has a heart-felt appreciation for the important things in life.

In his personal life, Russell cherishes the intimacy, trust, and devotion he feels in his close relationships with family and friends. He especially values his relationship with his lifetime partner, Jeanne Kuhlman—she is also a brilliant scientist, and they have been together for almost thirty years. It's so wonderful to see how emotional Russell becomes when he talks about Jeanne as his best friend and companion in every activity of his life.

Upon our introduction, I volunteered to help Russell clean his office, which was filled with stacks of journals, notebooks, files and loose pieces of paper. It was a challenge to clear his desk so that I could set up the microphones. We have all heard that geniuses tend to exist in cluttered environments. In Russell's case, how true this turned out to be.

I met with Russell at his office in the Princeton Plasma Laboratory located in Princeton, New Jersey:

Q: How does it make you feel knowing that you made such a profound contribution to your field?

A: It certainly makes me feel good. For me, the joy of science is almost a spiritual experience, finding out things about how the world works. Then that joy is doubled because you get a chance to share it with people.

Q: What does science mean to you, is it merely academic curiosity or a quest for something greater?

A: Science is very much part of the human condition. It's

curiosity. It's how you get to the truth. I can't think of anything more important than that. Science at its best moments is an aesthetic experience, ranging to a spiritual experience in the sense of being meaningful, in the sense that it's about having insight into something beautiful and wondrous.

Q: What goal did you have early on in your life? Was it academic knowledge, revolutionizing science, helping people?

A: I didn't really grow up with a planned goal in mind. I just knew that I liked science, and therefore, I was going to be a scientist. So I never thought "I'm going to do this because I'll win a prize. I'm going to do this because I want to show that I'm better than anybody else." I just thought, "I like to do this— so that's what I'll do."

Q: Are you as passionate today as you were when you first started?

A: It has had its ups and downs. The real world is often based on being a square peg for a square hole. The world is a structured place that likes people to be well-characterized and narrowly focused as to what they do and what they are. I've never really been quite that way.

Q: What does it take to be an inventor, discoverer or revolutionary thinker?

A: There's always some discipline involved. Science is about checking your answers— because having ideas is fine, but anybody can have ideas. It matters if you can prove it.

Q: How do you find the work that you love? Is it serendipity or must you search for it?

A: I think life is generally less predictable than a lot of people would like to think it is. Things happen due to odd coincidences and serendipity. Opportunities arise, and you have to be prepared to take advantage of them. On the other hand, as I reflect back, I feel I should have been more structured and disciplined in pursuing a career. You need a balance between the two.

Q: Do you think there are specific principles that have helped to make you successful at your work?

A: I think there are. For me being a scientist is not a career choice—it's a much deeper personal endeavor. Another important trait is honesty. I think that I'm a very honest person, and I insist on honesty from people. Being a decent individual flows in a large measure from that. I also think that honesty is connected with being a good scientist—having that connection with reality. It's important to know what's true, even if it doesn't make me happy.

Q: Is there anything else that has led to your achievement?

A: I've always had a do-it-yourself work ethic that I got from my father. I'm just going to go in, dig into it and figure it out.

Q: How about being able to overcome adversity in your life?

A: The thing that's most essential to me is having had the experience of adversity and knowing that I came out okay in the end. Remember that no matter how bad things look right now, you did get to the other side before. That's where you want to get to now—you just want to get to the other side.

Q: Can other people help us deal with adversity?

A: Yes, the right people. The wrong people [Laughing] are not what you want; in fact, they're often the cause of the adversity. But the right people are important.

Q: How essential is self-awareness?

A: I'm continually amazed at how non-introspective most people tend to be. That said, I can see the other side too. There is a danger of becoming too introspective, which can be debilitating. It's a trap I fall into every now and then.

Q: Faced with so many choices, is it difficult for you to decide which path to take in life?

A: Oh yes, I dither. [Laughing]

Q: How do you choose the right path?

A: With difficulty I guess. [Laughing]

Q: Is it about not being afraid to fail?

A: Right, you have to get passed being afraid to fail.

Q: In most of your decisions, are you one to follow you heart or your mind? Or is there a certain time for each one?

A: There's a certain time for each one. Actually, I'd say rather than a certain time for each one, they need to work together.

Q: How crucial is it to keep hope and be an optimist?

A: I think it is very important. It can be hard sometimes, especially for a person who's very reality-oriented, introspective and analytical. I can lose hope by seeing all the things that are wrong. Sometimes you have to just turn a blind eye to it and proceed.

Q: Think about the positive?

A: Think about the positive and just get into it—don't analyze it to death.

Q: Is it more important to be flexible so that you can adjust to the changes in life or steadfast so that you can weather the storm that changes bring?

A: Part of leadership is figuring out when to be flexible and using that flexibility to great advantage to deal with unexpected circumstances. But, in other situations, it's being able to hunker down and say, "This is what we're doing. I don't care how it looks, and what everybody else says—just do it."

Q: You're an extremely reflective and independent person. I'm curious to know your thoughts on society. What kind of pressures have you felt from society?

A: Popular culture, particularly nowadays, I find most of it reprehensible and uninteresting. The focus of society on money, power and aggressiveness. I can't relate to it, and I try to ignore it.

Q: Is it possible to keep your individuality and fight off those pressures?

A: I think it is, and I think it's very important. You should identify with who you are and what's really important in life, not with who somebody else is, and especially not with what the media hypes as being trendy or cool.

Q: Do you think society's values have changed during the course of your life?

A: I think they have, some for better and some for worse.

Q: In what way?

A: Our society has become more tolerant in many ways, which is a good thing. However, I think there is more dominance of the mass media culture, which is a very huge negative. It's sending messages about how people relate and live their life with an intensity that's unprecedented. I think it's very destructive. Sex has been trivialized and commercialized. I'm not calling for censorship. I'm just saying society has to have the maturity to push back.

Q: What aspects about our society fill you with hope?

A: It's being old enough to have seen societal swings. You start to almost believe in the fact that society is self-correcting. We always swing too far in one direction, but then at some point it starts to come back.

Q: Where do you think society and the world will be thirty years from now?

A: Oh boy, that's a good one. To be honest, I tend to flip-flop on that. Sometimes I think this will all work out.

Q: I hope so! To finish off on a philosophical note, what do you believe is the meaning of life?

A: I think there is a lot of meaning. I think that having a purpose in life is very important. Part of it is other people—having honest, meaningful, real relationships with other people.

Q: Enjoying the time that we have here?

A: Right, enjoying the time that we have here, and along with that, having spirituality. For me, spirituality is in the natural world and aesthetics, having meaningful experiences with the natural world.

Q: After everything is said and done, how do you want to be remembered?

A: As a nice guy, someone who people can trust and respect.

Talking with Russell, one is struck by the sincerity in his eyes, warmness in his heart, and purity in his soul. Russell's life is a perpetual search for truth and honesty. He detests pretentiousness, because he believes it distracts people from the important things in life. The important things in Russell's life include having close relationships with other people, appreciating nature, partaking in science and generally valuing life. More than anything, Russell despises deception, and those individuals in society who get ahead by disregarding ethics, and disrespecting others. While Russell seeks to remain an optimist, he is disappointed to see society saturated with immorality, thoughtlessness and an overall lack of civility.

Russell believes it is important to know what's true, even if it doesn't make you happy. Although he is an accomplished Nobel Laureate and one of the most acclaimed scientists in the world, he frequently acknowledges and shares many of his personal regrets, drawbacks and mistakes. Russell only feels comfortable presenting himself as he really is, without social fronts or defense mechanisms. His frankness and simplicity give him a human element that makes him easy to identify with. Russell explains that his honesty makes him a good scientist. I would suggest that it makes him a good human being.

Why has honesty become so rare in our society? In a never-ending race to impress one another, people are often preoccupied by hiding parts of themselves, or making themselves out to be something that they're not. Politicians lie, businessmen cheat, and the mass media distorts the truth. Our culture at times seems to have become comfortable with deception. The unfortunate but understandable result has been an increasingly cynical and untrusting public. And for what? Those who engage in dishonesty for financial gain, do so at the expense of the greater good, and ultimately our society is the victim. It doesn't make any sense. Look at Russell, who has achieved what so many others desire by pursuing a simple yet noble goal—to be "a nice guy, someone who people can trust and respect." Could you imagine what kind of world there would be if everyone approached life this way?

—CHAPTER 15—

PERSEVERANCE

DELFORD SMITH

Things sometimes look bleak, and it's so tempting to just quit. At these hardest of times, how do you overcome adversity?

Delford "Del" Smith is the chairman and 100 percent owner of Evergreen Aviation, one of the largest privately-held companies in the United States, with over $600 million in yearly revenues. In 1960, Del founded Evergreen with a plan to use helicopters for various agriculture and forestry projects, as well as firefighting and humanitarian relief missions. Since then, Evergreen's business has expanded to include operations in aircraft cargo, chartering, repairs, ground-handling, sales, and leasing, along with its endeavors in forestry and farming. As originally intended, his business includes a nonprofit humanitarian relief organization, which helps fight problems like disease, hunger and poverty all over the world.

Throughout his life, Del has had to overcome adversity. After losing both his parents at birth, he was forced to begin his life at an orphanage. When he was two years old, he was adopted by step-parents. Tragically, his step-father died shortly afterwards, and as a result, his loving step-mother, "Grandma Smith," raised him on her own. Grandma Smith was a poor, struggling laborer, and Del felt a responsibility to contribute financially from a very young age. He began working at eight years old, and, by the time he was eleven, Del had saved up enough money for a down payment on a house. From that point on, he made every mortgage payment until the home was paid in full. He was even able to keep paying the mortgage during college, while he was funding his own education.

Del's adversity continued into adulthood. After an unsuccessful first marriage, he was left to raise his two sons alone. He chose not to remarry while the boys were young, perceiving that this might have a negative affect on their upbringing. With both his sons and his business growing, Del had to perform a delicate balancing act. Despite the many challenges, Del was an amazing father, and the kids grew up to be terrific men. However, that's when real tragedy struck. In 1995, his eldest son, Michael, was killed in a car accident.

Although the grief has been unbearable at times, Del has always battled through the adversity in his life and found a way to move on. Over the years, his Christian faith has been a bastion of strength. By using Evergreen as a vehicle for philanthropy, he has been able to dedicate his life to a greater purpose. In recent years, Del has found true love with his new wife, Maria. Since the tragic accident, she has brought much joy into his life.

I met with Del at Evergreen Aviation headquarters in McMinnville, Oregon:

Q: Have you felt a pressure to achieve extraordinary things in your life?

A: If I did, it was self-imposed. To this day, I still get up at five and come to the company's daily seven o'clock meetings. At age seventy-three, I feel guilty as hell if I sleep in.

Q: What does that stem from? What motivates you at your core?

A: I think if you're the leader, you've got to lead by example.

Q: You've been able to do and accomplish so much in your life. In the early stages of your career, would you have conceived that all this would have been possible?

A: No, I think you grow by steps and plateaus. I don't think that when you're twenty-five or thirty, you have a clear vision of what it involves.

Q: What were your original goals and intentions?

A: I became interested in business, and wanted to build it with the right business philosophy—to be responsible to God's will. I still work at it. (I also wanted to) be the best of the best.

Q: How did you make that transfer from working for somebody else to starting your own business?

A: I knew at a very, very young age that I wanted to work for myself. [Laughing] My wife says that it's a good thing, because nobody else would probably employ me. [Laughing]

Q: Were you ambitious out of necessity?

A: Oh yes, I could top most of your poor stories. We were poor.

Q: What kind of effect did that have on the rest of your life?

A: Well, I've been extremely poor and I've had material comfort and I guess I prefer material comfort. [Laughing] No, I'll give you a serious answer. It makes you want to achieve. I think being hungry makes a difference.

Q: And you felt a responsibility to provide?

A: I did. I came out of an orphanage and the mother that adopted me was a saint. Grandma Smith had to work hard to raise me. She wasn't blessed with a rich education, so she had to work hard for every dime that she earned. This lady taught me so much—she used to say, "Success is ninety percent action and ten percent talk."

Q: She sounded like she was a very inspirational figure.

A: Oh yes. She would also say, "Resolve what you are and perform without fail what you resolve." I still use that one on a frequent basis.

Q: It sounds like you really loved her.

A: Oh yes. When I was eleven years old, I bought her a home. That's a true story.

Q: How were you able to do that at eleven years old?

A: Well, interest in those days was two and a half percent, and I delivered a lot of newspapers. I had two routes in the morning and one after school. Both of us saved. She taught me to be frugal. I think by the time I was eleven I had a hundred dollars.

Q: And that was enough for a down-payment back then?

A: Yes, way, way back in the forties.

Q: Because homes only cost a few thousand dollars?

A: They would cost four thousand. I never missed a payment on that, all the way through high school and college.

Q: Even while you were studying in college and working to pay off your education?

A: Yes, and I did work hard to pay off my education.

Q: What has your family meant to you over the years?

A: It's your purpose for living. That's why I worked so hard. I wanted to do something that would make my kids proud. I wanted to be a responsible father. I also knew that I was going to have to take care of my mother. So I needed to be making enough to look after her and still look after the family.

Q: So all the riches that you acquire in your life don't matter without your family?

A: No, as a matter of fact, the riches really don't matter.

Q: Over the years, as your business has grown successful, has it changed your life much?

A: No. My wife, Maria, changed my life. She makes me dress better. [Laughing]

Q: Getting back to more personal philosophy, what does it take to be successful?

A: I'd say passion and a desire to do something. And I think adversity can be a launching pad. First of all, you have to set goals—goal-setting is goal-getting. We set goals here every Monday morning. Then we check them the following Monday as to whether they were accomplished. Forgiveness is a wonderful virtue, but it's not policy here. [Laughing] They have to sit here and go into confession. [Laughing]

Q: And you're very demanding?

A: I think I'm a dove. [Laughing]

Q: So performance is very important to you?

A: The only thing that counts in life is performance. I have a zero tolerance for excuses. I think they're a total waste. Time should be spent solving the problem, not blaming each other. The other thing I learned is that if your mind can conceive and believe, you can achieve. I really believe that. If you think you can't, you can't. If you think you can, you can.

Q: Are you a true believer in making your own destiny?

A: Absolutely. Coming out of an orphanage causes part of that. Because you don't know your heritage, you don't know what you inherited. I think you have to make your destiny. I was the class president every year in my first through eighth grade, likewise in high school and college. I then wanted to be a responsible leader in the military. I preach that around here—I still think leadership is the rarest talent on earth. There are more sheep then there are shepherds.

Q: You were born in an orphanage, adopted by a family that didn't have much money, and then, shortly afterwards, your adopted-father passed away. How are you able to overcome adversity time and time again?

A: Just make up your mind never to quit. We have had some real battles. I mean if we got into those, we'd have you crying. [Laughing] Just believe in yourself and believe in your Maker. Faith is an element, and hope. However, you can't take hope to the bank. [Laughing] That doesn't work. [Laughing]

Q: Even though you can't take it to the bank, how crucial is it to keep hope and be an optimist in overcoming adversity?

A: I think hope is one of the best friends you'll have in your life, but it has to be practical. I think the virtue of persistence is very important. Ninety percent of the sales are made on the fifth call. Only ten percent of salesmen are persistent enough to make that fifth call. So that's why ten percent get ninety percent of the business. Yes, you must have hope!

Q: So like they say, "attitude is everything"?

A: You have to be positive. It's the old joke about the really optimistic kid and the really pessimistic kid and the parents who didn't know what to do. So they said, "Let's just shower the pessimist with Christmas toys. And the optimist, we'll fill his bedroom with horse manure." So Christmas morning the two kids jumped out of bed, and the pessimist found skates, kites, musical instruments and sports gear. But the bat was too heavy, the whistle wouldn't whistle and the skates wouldn't skate—same pessimist. The little optimist went in there and said, "Hey dad, with all this horse manure, there's got to be a pony somewhere." [Laughing]

Q: You're obviously an optimist, but have you made a lot of mistakes along the way?

A: Oh, we don't have time. [Laughing] Yes, it's a learning process. You got to dust them off, get back up and keep going. Adversity can be a launching pad for something bigger and better.

Q: So you don't let mistakes get you down. How about cynics? Do cynics affect you?

A: Hell no! They spur me on. (You have to) prove them wrong.

Q: Has that motivated you?

A: Yes, if you want the truth.

Q: You have managed to become successful while always remaining true to a high standard of integrity. How do you accomplish both?

A: I think you have to be honest with your Maker, honest with people you deal with and honest with yourself. I think that takes a pretty frequent check.

Q: Besides integrity, what are the other principles of good leadership?

A: I think that a leader should be a teacher. I think the mission needs to be clear. It's helping people set goals. It's being responsible and putting the right team together. It's helping people believe in themselves. It's teaching people to be team players. It's teaching them to be enthusiastic.

Q: Do you believe that being in a position of leadership gives you more responsibility?

A: I think you're the servant; you're not the king. You may be perceived as the king, but you're really busting your buttons to serve others. I don't think that corporate America has done right in the last ten years. I think that they can be setting much better examples.

Q: How do you reconcile the fact that there's so many people in society, so many successful businesspeople, who do not show good integrity?

A: It makes me sick. There isn't a justice system. I don't think there's any one guy in that Oregon State Penitentiary that is as bad as some of these bankers that were ripping people off.

Q: What would you tell the younger generation, who see these things happening in our society and could be influenced by them?

A: I'd probably tell them to watch out for the bad. Don't be over-trusting.

Q: You have to watch out for the bad people? Do you have to choose very carefully who you associate with?

A: The older you get, the more you know that. But even Jesus had Judas.

Q: It's hard to do. It seems like there are many dishonest people in society. Have society's values changed during the course of your life?

A: Yes, absolutely! I think they're the bunk. [Laughing] Are we on the air? [Laughing] I think there's a lot of falseness.

Q: What do you think are some of the biggest problems with our society today?

A: I think society places the wrong value on fame and fortune. There's a lot of pretentiousness in society today.

Q: If you had the power to change one thing in the world, what would it be?

A: It would relate to the Golden Rule. We need a more honest and responsible world—more accountability, more honesty and more virtue.

Q: To conclude things, let's get really philosophical. What's the secret to being happy and fulfilled in your life?

A: I think having an active, industrious life. Love people, love your family, do things for others and do something worthwhile. Stay positive. There are more people on earth that will put you down than pick you up—don't listen to any of them.

Q: Do you have any regrets over the years?

A: I think anybody who's honest has got to admit there are things that they could of done, should of done and would of done differently. I don't let these things make me sick. I think you got to have a healthy discontent for the present and always try to make the future better than the present.

Q: What do you believe is the meaning of life?

A: Your beliefs as far as your Maker—that's obviously a big part of it. I want to believe that there's life after death. I don't think it's just dust and ashes.

Q: How do you want to be remembered?

A: I don't want any vanity. I just think that the reward in life is that you serve God and do something good for mankind.

It's inspirational to witness Delford's unwavering strength and undying spirit. Despite his many hardships, he always finds a way to persevere. He has an uncanny ability to overcome adversity—from being born in an orphanage, to growing up destitute, to raising his two children alone, to building a business, to suffering the death of his beloved son. Del is a warrior, who believes that life is a constant battle. His faith in God and belief in himself encourage him to keep moving forward.

Adversity doesn't keep Del down; in fact, he uses many of his struggles as a launching pad for something greater. Growing up poor only made him more ambitious. Facing business challenges only encouraged him to work harder. Making mistakes along the way did not discourage him, but allowed him to learn. Talking with cynics only spurred him on to prove them wrong. No matter what the storm brings in, Del always maintains his resolve to never quit.

How many times have all of us been overwhelmed with fear, insecurity, failure and tragedy? How many times have we felt the urge to stop? Life isn't easy. There are always pitfalls and problems. It's natural to be afraid. It's natural to get upset. However, we have to do everything we can to keep moving forward. We owe it to ourselves to go on. If you are able to survive the bad times, you will eventually find the good. Always keep hope. Always keep fighting. Ask Del and he'll tell you—adversity is meant to be overcome!

—Chapter 16—

Strength & Leadership

James Kimsey

What does it take to be a leader? Where can you find strength in times of trouble?

In 1982, James "Jim" Kimsey was an up-and-coming, successful entrepreneur, when he heard from a friend about a struggling technology company that desperately needed assistance. After careful consideration, Jim decided to invest. Since the company was located near his home in Washington D.C., he started spending more and more time on the project. Taking the lead, he saved the company from bankruptcy, reorganized it, and renamed it Quantum Computer Services. After a few initial attempts to sell the company, James decided to stay on for the long haul as its chairman and CEO. In 1990, Quantum changed its name to America Online or AOL, which most of us know today as the multi-billion dollar Internet provider and mass media conglomerate.

Jim remained in the top position of AOL until 1996, when he voluntarily passed on the torch. The success of his company brought Jim more money than he could spend in ten lifetimes.

Since money was no longer an issue, Jim realized he was in a position to pursue the greater good through social contribution. In 1997, with this goal in mind, Jim started the Kimsey Foundation, a charitable, non-profit organization that works to alleviate social problems around the world. Through the Kimsey Foundation, which he runs to this day, Jim has done everything from negotiating with world leaders and implementing humanitarian relief, to promoting education and helping build communities.

Jim was educated at West Point. Upon graduation, he served in the military for eight years, and fought in three tours of duty, one in the Dominican Republic and two in Vietnam. While serving in Vietnam, Jim managed numerous troops and witnessed much bloodshed. By the time he left the military in 1969, James had earned the rank of major. He had also gained an understanding of what he wanted out of life—the challenge of new experiences, financial independence, control of his own life, and the ability to make a positive contribution to society.

In his personal life, Jim is most proud of his three sons, one of whom works with him at the Kimsey Foundation. Jim values close relationships with friends and family. Despite his tough exterior, Jim deeply cares about other people and the world around him, and feels a profound responsibility to work for the greater good.

I met with Jim at Kimsey Foundation Headquarters in Washington D.C. His top-floor office is next door to the White House with a terrace overlooking the President's gardens:

Q: How essential is self-awareness in our lives?

A: I think it's critical. I think it's very important. "An unexamined life is not worth living." If you don't understand yourself, then you're going to have a hard time understanding others.

Q: Faced with so many choices in your life, how do you choose the direction that is right for you?

A: Well, I think everybody is essentially doing what they want to do, what they've chosen to do. The way you are in life is the sum total of every choice you've made since birth. Everybody on this earth has tons of choices every single day.

Q: How does fate figure into that?

A: Any time anybody says that they didn't have a choice because they just got dealt a bad hand, it's simply not true. Now the recognition of this fact, because it is a fact, is extraordinarily important. When you get up in the morning you can do any bloody thing you choose to do. That's why you're sitting here right now. Everybody on this earth, right this minute, is doing what they've chosen to do. Once you understand that's the case, then you start looking at things differently. You start saying I could be doing this or I could be doing that. Why am I doing this and why am I doing that? Where do I want to end up? Many people say it's easier to not confront those kinds of issues. It's easier to settle into a routine. It's easier to blame the universe, or consequences, or your neighbors, or God knows what.

Q: How did you make things happen in your life? You've been able to be successful at everything that you do, and you end up in amazing positions. Is it because you put yourself in these positions?

A: There are no accidents. I think you tend to position yourself in ways that eventually determine your outcome.

Q: What were your original intentions and goals when you started your business career?

A: My business career didn't start until I was thirty, because I was in the army until that point. My goal was to get money out of the way so it wasn't an issue. That way I could focus on other things.

Q: How did you get the vision to start a company like AOL? What does it take to be a visionary?

A: I think you have to be able to envision what others might not be able to see. You think ahead enough to have a firm idea in your mind about what could happen. It's being able to see the potential in any given activity.

Q: Do you use your intuition to guide you? Is that where you get your vision?

A: I think that a lot of times you have to let your instincts guide you. In life, there are some things that you just have to do. You will not regret those things that you did, only the things that you haven't done.

Q: So what did it take to build such a large business like AOL?

A: Leadership and the ability to motivate people to do what you want them to do. You also have to understand what the endgame is. What the goal is in any particular endeavor.

Q: Were there specific personality traits that you possessed that helped you in the process?

A: Positive attitude. You have to be an optimist, and you have to be willing to take chances. You have to do some thought about what you want. Sometimes you have to risk security and stability to make those things happen, and that's not for everybody. Some people don't feel comfortable doing that.

Q: So your ability to take risks has helped you to achieve things in life?

A: Most everything.

Q: Is that something you're born with?

A: I think it's part of a congenital predisposition on the one hand, but I think it's something you also can nurture and train yourself to do better. You need a fair amount of confidence in your ability to handle unforeseen circumstances, because it's definitely not going to turn out the way you planned. You have to be quick enough and resourceful enough to take advantage of the opportunity.

Q: How about your ability to overcome adversity? How instrumental has that been to your success?

A: Well, if I didn't have any (adversity), I'd go find some. I think life without challenges is dull. I've always been drawn to that sort of thing. I volunteered to go to Vietnam the first time in 1965. Obstacles and challenges energize me. I enjoy them.

Q: Have you made a lot of mistakes along the way?

A: I've made lots of mistakes and you have to accept that. But I'm confident that I can recover from my mistakes. The trick is when you make a mistake, recognize it and correct it. Don't act like it didn't happen. Do everything you can to correct it!

Q: You have such inner-strength. How did you get this way? Did the fact that your family struggled financially early in your life influence you for the rest of your life?

A: I worked since I could remember.

Q: So it instilled this great work ethic in you?

A: There were always kids that had a hell of a lot more money than we did—we had zero. So it was probably a motivating factor. But I never felt poor, just they had money and I didn't. I noticed the preoccupation that people had with money. This car is better than that car, etc…I said, "Boy, what a nice thing it would be to just get passed all that, to a point where you didn't care about money." The only way to do that is get a bunch of it.

Q: What did your years at West Point teach you?

A: There are no excuses. You accept that, if you're the leader. You're responsible for everything that your organization does. That creates an internal process of thinking ahead.

Q: It makes you live your life by a different standard, a higher standard?

A: I think so. There's a lot of blame cast by leaders when something doesn't turn out right. If you're the captain of the Titanic, you should know that the damn iceberg is going to be there. Period!

Q: What impact did your military service have on you?

A: The training to be a leader and the discipline of having to live that kind of lifestyle. I had three combat tours, one in the Dominican Republic and two in Vietnam. Nothing can intimidate me coming into the business world. What are you going to say or do (to intimidate me)?

Q: Did your time in the military teach you that by being in a position of leadership, you have a greater sense of responsibility?

A: Absolutely, the more power you have, the more responsibility you have.

Q: With all your various experiences—military, work, family—what's the greatest thing that you've learned during the course of your lifetime?

A: Life experience teaches you many things about human nature primarily. Your ability to be a leader is a function of how you interact with other human beings.

Q: That certainly requires some understanding of human nature. Talking about human nature, what are your views on society? Looking at society today, are there aspects that fill you with hope?

A: People talk about how the world is getting worse and worse. I don't think so. Years ago, I lived in a little village in Vietnam. Those people didn't have anything; they were dirt poor. I lived in that village for a year, and got to know those people. They were happy. Oh yes, they were happy as hell! Their lives revolved around their little social interactions, and all the stuff they did.

Q: Happier than a lot of wealthy Americans?

A: Absolutely! Their lives are simple but every day was a full day. Most of these folks in the world are not as bad off as we think they are. Most of them live happy, productive lives.

Q: If you had the power to change one thing in the world, what would it be?

A: Take away tribal enmity, which is the root of all these conflicts. For a hundred years, the world has sort of lived under this world cataclysm, which included the world wars followed by the threat of nuclear holocaust. Now, the Berlin wall has come down and the threat of nuclear annihilation is gone. You'd think that the world would be a fuzzier, warmer and nicer place. However, we have more refugees now than ever in history. There is tribal warfare that has exploded around the world.

Q: So if you had the ability to do one thing, you'd erase history?

A: [Laughing] Well, this sort of tribal enmity, this tribal hatred that exists. How deep it runs. But it's the nature of man if it was ever thus.

Q: You have faced many challenges and hardships in your life and overcome them all. What's the secret to being happy and fulfilled in life?

A: I think being honest with yourself, sometimes brutally. [Laughing] If you're not honest with yourself, then on some level you know it—I don't think your life will be happy. Life is never one hundred percent a bowl of cherries. There are going to be ups and downs. Bad things happen. People that you care about get in trouble, have a problem, or get sick. However, if you feel good about who you are and what you're doing, everything can be improved upon.

Q: What do you believe is the meaning of life?

A: I think there's somebody bigger and better than us. When I started the Kimsey Foundation, we had a company meeting. I tried to explain to all the employees what the purpose of the foundation was going to be. I said, "I think that when you go through life, most people make deals with somebody somewhere. If I get through this test I'll be a better student. If I get out of this battle alive, I'll be a better person. If I get out of this bankruptcy threat, I'll be a better citizen. Some day when you get to where it is you think you wanted to be, this big voice goes—*well, all these little promises you've been making, well?*" I think I have a strong sense of debt. You know the old tale about if much is given, much is expected? I've been given a lot.

Q: Do you think life's about working toward a greater purpose?

A: It's something I enjoy doing. It's something I feel will hopefully add value and help the world be a better place. There are only two things that you're going to think about when you're dying—not about money, not about how big your company was, or any of that stuff. You're going to think about your relationships with your kids and family. You're also going to think about whether the world is a better place because you were here. At that point, if the answer is no, it's too late.

Through his every word and action, Jim demonstrates strength and leadership ability. Among other experiences, his military background has given him the confidence to withstand any challenge. After overcoming bloodshed and death on the battlefield, nothing can be done to scare or dishearten Jim, or force him to compromise his strong values and integrity. He'll stand on his own, set an example and assume full responsibility. He'll face any challenge and overcome any adversity.

Not only is James Kimsey able to overcome obstacles and problems, he actually invites them. He admits that he is reinvigorated in the face of hardship. What does it take to have such strength? For Jim, it is his vast experience in life that has eliminated the fears, insecurities, and weaknesses that plague many of us. He has fought wars, started businesses, attained titles, accumulated wealth, raised a family, and given back to society. Every experience he collects, every challenge he confronts, and every adversity he overcomes, leads to greater strength and leadership ability.

All of us are forced to confront fears at some point in our lives. Even James Kimsey has been afraid or uncomfortable at some point in his past. In our own way, we all need to experience a variety of situations in life in order to gain the confidence to overcome our fears. The trick is not to let fear stop you from doing whatever it is that you want to do. Over time, it gets easier. With each new challenge, you gain confidence and courage, and eventually nothing seems insurmountable.

—Chapter 17—

Charisma

Linda Alvarado

Can a good sense of humor work to your advantage?
How far does personality take you?

Linda Alvarado is the founder and chairman of Alvarado Construction, one of the largest construction companies in the United States. Her projects have included the Denver Broncos Stadium, Colorado Convention Center and Hotel, Denver International Airport, and numerous high-rise buildings. In addition to her construction business, she is also a major owner of the Colorado Rockies Major League Baseball team, as well as over a hundred fast food franchises, including Pizza Huts, Taco Bells and Kentucky Fried Chicken restaurants.

When I came across Linda's story, I found it intriguing that a woman from a poor, Hispanic family was able to thrive in such traditionally male-dominated industries, particularly construction. In 1976, Linda's parents mortgaged their home in order to give her the $2500 loan she needed to start her construction company. Linda had been turned down by every financial lender she had approached because the bankers had been skeptical that a young Hispanic woman would be capable of running a construction company. Over time, she would prove them all wrong. From her humble beginnings, installing concrete sidewalks, curbs or gutters, or doing any other job she could get to pay back her parents, Linda has become one of the most prosperous people in America.

Linda has been married to her husband, Robert, for almost twenty years, and they have three children. Robert works with Linda, managing the restaurant branch of their business. The two support each other in their home and work lives, and together they do their best to balance family life with the demands of business. Linda is also an acclaimed philanthropist, who especially enjoys contributing her time to helping children, minorities and women. Linda is known in the Denver area for taking disadvantaged children to baseball games, and providing special work opportunities for struggling women. In recognition of her many accomplishments and contributions, she has recently been inducted into the National Women's Hall of Fame.

I met with Linda at the Alvarado Construction offices in Denver, Colorado:

Q: You own a construction company. You own multiple restaurants chains. You own a professional baseball team. You were nominated into the Women's Hall of Fame this year. Could you have ever expected that you would be where you are today?

A: [Laughing] I grew up in a relatively "small" Hispanic family. There were only six in my family. I had all brothers, no sisters. My parents were from very modest backgrounds, but they were very optimistic people. Growing up, I think my family had an interesting dynamic. We did not know that we were poor or at least we did not perceive that we were. I think one of my parent's greatest gifts was empowering their kids to see the best in themselves.

Q: In the beginning, you had problems finding contracts to build bus shelters and pave roads. How do you go from that to building high-rises, convention centers and airports?

A: I know when you're in school, people will say, "You need to plan your career. You need to study and apply yourself to be successful." While preparation and planning are helpful, I also believe the theory that not all great careers are planned! I started by acquiring a license to install small concrete jobs.

Q: But how did you become so successful?

A: Part of it might be that I grew up with all brothers; I was not really treated differently than my brothers. It was a competitive family. Although I may have been successful doing many different things, I had a passion for building forts in our backyard and playing sports even as a girl, it seems natural to me.

Q: You go into construction, which is a male-dominated business, and eventually you buy a baseball franchise, which again is a male-dominated arena. How are you able to keep overcoming this gender barrier?

A: I don't think I have to act like a male to thrive in a male-dominated environment. One has to be well-grounded, and you must have a strong knowledge base of what the industry is all about. Most importantly, I think it's getting along with people and building teams that can work together to achieve positive results.

Q: Did you overcome the gender barrier because you just had that much confidence in yourself?

A: No, no, no. It's hard to be confident when you are the only woman on the construction site.

Q: And yet you did it. What would you advise other people who feel that there's some kind of bias against them in the workforce?

A: I strongly believe you have to take your dreams seriously. Do not be discouraged by others' perception. One needs to be very resourceful, have a great sense of humor, meet people and get involved. I think too many people are waiting for opportunities to come to them.

Q: Your parents gave you a $2500 loan to start off the business, because you weren't able to get a loan from a bank at the time. Did that put a great pressure on you to succeed?

A: Yes. If I had not paid that money back, my parents would have lost their house. But whether I succeeded or failed, I knew they still would love me. The fact that they had put their life savings on the line for me—that is something that really encouraged me going forward. I wanted to not only pay them back, but to show them that all the sacrifices they had made for their children did pay off. And they have.

Q: How are you able to overcome adversity?

A: Well, sometimes you win, sometimes you do not get the job, but you never lose. I can live with that. No matter how good you are, you're going to fail at times. During those times, you need to learn from the experience, redirect your focus, try another approach, and never give up.

Q: As a woman, how do you balance work with family?

A: I think there is no way to perfectly balance it. It is what I call an opportunity cost. I have to be in San Francisco because I am proposing a very large project, but it is also the mother-daughter Brownie banquet that night. I can't go to the mother-daughter Brownie banquet. It is a family opportunity lost for me. It is clear that one cannot have everything all the time. You have to find a balance.

Q: You have been married for nearly two decades. What's the secret to finding the right spouse?

A: You're a bond trader, you tell me. [Laughing] I don't know. I think it's different for everybody. So I don't know if there is a formula, but I believe it is one of the most important decisions one makes as it impacts one's personal and career decisions. I do not think that one size fits all. I tell my son that, "Gone are the days that you choose the woman; women are going to choose you."

Q: Family seems to be extremely important to you. What does it take to have a good, strong family?

A: We should have some liquor here for this. [Laughing] I am not sure that I can speak to what works for everyone else.

Q: Well, how about what works for you?

A: First, it is respect for everyone in the family, placing your trust in them and their trust also in you. Having a sense of humor is important, since we often disagree. There is not a shortage of opinions in our family, but it is important to recognize the best in other people, even though they are not as perfect as you! [Laughing]

Q: Can I interview your husband to confirm this? [Laughing] We should probably get back to discussing your career before you really get in trouble. [Laughing] How were you able to find the kind of work that you love?

A: For me, it has to be something that is challenging. If you asked me when I was younger, would I be a contractor? I would not have known that. If you had asked me when I was in business for ten years, would I own a baseball team? I would not have known that. If you asked me today, what will I be doing in the future? I do not know. But what I do not want is to be narrow in my thinking. I want to have the ability to make choices, and that is something that historically women have lacked.

Q: Do you have to make it happen for yourself?

A: In business, you work hard to position yourself. Then, when the opportunity comes, one has to act in order to not miss it. To a great extent, I believe one creates their own destiny. Sometimes you hit a wall. Sometimes you would not get there on the first attempt, but you look for another way around the obstacle to get back on track.

Q: Did this determination develop from your early life experiences? Growing up, your family was very poor. You didn't even have indoor plumbing. You had a stove as a heater. How did that affect your future thinking?

A: We did not own a car. My father would walk to work, and my mother hauled water from the irrigation ditch to wash our clothes. But my parents would say, "Look, there will be people that are better looking than you, taller than you, who don't have Hispanic blood—you are going to feel at some point in time that they have some kind of advantage over you. Those are excuses, they are not reasons for achieving."

Q: I think it also instilled in you a never-give-up attitude.

A: When somebody knocks your ideas down, you need to get up and keep fighting to keep your focus.

Q: Who were your greatest role models early on in your life?

A: My sixth grade teacher, Loy Sue Siegebtgaker. She had this little book club. After school, we would read these biographies. She encouraged us to start reading about other people's experiences. Reading those biographies helped me understand a world that I might never have thought I would be part of. In a way, you learn from these biographies, which provided both good and bad experiences, people's feelings and perspectives, and how they worked to overcome obstacles.

Q: So your sixth grade teacher made a big impression on you?

A: The thing that I will always remember is that my teacher said,

"Work is fun." She said, "Men go to work and they say, my gosh, it was a tough day out there." Then she would laugh and say, "What they do not tell you about is how much fun it is to work. How they thrive at work in brainstorming and solving problems."

Q: With all your experience in school, family and work, what are the most important things you've learned during your lifetime?

A: My mother advised me in Spanish, to start small but think big. I've also learned that it is really not all about brains or money; it is really all about working with people.

Q: Have you been motivated to succeed throughout your life?

A: There is a sense of wanting to succeed, no doubt. I dreamed of someday building high-rises. Today, I build high-rises, prisons, convention centers, and stadiums.

Q: Do you have any regrets, in your work or personal life?

A: I do not believe it does any good to dwell on regrets. Learn from them. Responses such as "I should of, would of and could of" are not very helpful.

Q: What do you believe is the meaning of life?

A: I don't know. Are you sure you weren't a psychology major? [Laughing] I think people change throughout their life.

Q: How about more specifically, what are the most important things in life for you?

A: Having choices and being involved in community activities, not just things that benefit only me. I am intrigued by other people's experiences and life stories, which point to the fact that success in life is really not just about money.

Q: How essential is self-awareness?

A: I am probably my biggest critique. My husband never hears me say that. [Laughing] I am extremely tough on myself.

Q: Would you say you are one to follow your heart or your mind?

A: [Laughing] I think I follow my head. I'm analytical but not to the point of paralysis.

Q: And yet you're open-minded?

A: Oh yes, I believe that everybody who works for me is smarter than I am. Just ask them and they will tell you just how much smarter they are. [Laughing]

Q: What's the secret to staying passionate in your life?

A: Are you talking about personal (life)? [Laughing] What works for me is realizing that every day is a new day. I look at it knowing that things will go wrong inevitably, but I don't dwell on it, which for all of us is easier said than done.

Q: How would you advise other people to become successful and achieve great things in their lives?

A: I think you have to have a good sense of direction, a good sense of ethical values, and as I have said before, a good sense of humor. Practice! Practice! Practice! And then, risk-taking! Risk-taking! Risk-taking! Being comfortable in taking risk really enables us to find out what we are capable of achieving.

Q: What's the secret to having a happy and fulfilled life?

A: [Laughing] Your interview is for philosophers or poets, certainly not contractors! Contractors believe that good days are those with no rain, and no mud. I don't know what the secret is for a happy life. Maybe having a good hair day. [Laughing] I mean how would you define that? It would be different for everyone, as it should be.

Q: How about overall?

A: Overall, I feel some sense of accomplishment. I am pleased that I have been able to come from a point where as a Hispanic woman nobody gave me much of a chance to achieve in business.

Q: Is there a certain impact you want to have on the world?

A: Perhaps I will be viewed as somebody who has taken nontraditional paths. Breaking the stereotypes is something we must all work toward.

Q: What in your life do you have the greatest love for?

A: My husband of course, and family. However, a little piece of my heart also belongs to Cheetos! [Laughing] Projects come and projects go. Life is about people.

Q: If you had the power to change one thing, what would it be?

A: Cheetos would have fewer calories. [Laughing]

It was a delight to be in Linda's company; the charisma and wonderful sense of humor she showed me are the same qualities that have led to her success. Her personality helps her build human relationships. It breaks the ice, allowing people to feel comfortable in her presence, and opens the door for communication. More importantly, it makes others want to be around her and share in the fun. As Linda explains, it is the relationships we form with people that ultimately create our success.

Linda's charisma and sense of humor also help make her resilient. Her ability to laugh at her mistakes, failures, and other adversities keeps her moving forward rather than dwelling on the past.

Working at a construction site was not easy for Linda in the beginning. Men on the site were not always respectful or accommodating to her, and sometimes there was even blatant sexual harassment. Some men would openly mock her, and others would draw obscene sketches of her in the portable bathrooms. Although offended, Linda shrugged it off and even joked about it. At least, she says, her colleagues always made her look really beautiful. They were also respectful enough to draw her wearing a hard hat, proving that, even when naked, she was always abiding of the safety regulations.

We are living in a society that has become very serious. Between our work schedules and family obligations, we have too many worries and too little time. It seems we have lost something along the way. It is during times like these, when charisma and humor are hardest to find, that the right personality may be the most valuable asset in the world.

—CHAPTER 18—

RESPONSIBILITY

WILSON GREATBATCH

Do I have a responsibility to help society? Do I have
responsibility to be a good, honest person?
Do I have the ability to make a difference?

Wilson "Bill" Greatbatch is arguably the greatest living inventor of our time. His first and most famous invention was the implantable heart pacemaker. As a result of this work, millions of lives have been saved, but for Bill this was only the beginning of an innovative career. Today, after a lifetime of work, he holds more than 300 domestic and international patents. Bill has been presented the National Medal of Technology and inducted into the Inventors Hall of Fame.

Business has been an important component of Bill's life. Never losing sight of reality, he has always tried to find practical applications for his inventions. With his pacemaker technology, Bill helped build Medtronic into the multibillion-dollar company it is today. Then Bill founded Wilson Greatbatch Technologies Inc., which originally sold another one of his patented technologies, the lithium battery. Today, like Medtronic, this corporation is traded on the New York Stock Exchange, and has a valuation of approximately one billion dollars. He also has founded other successful companies that have marketed his innovations, including his newest venture, Greatbatch Enterprises Corporation. Now eighty-four years old, Bill continues to manage this company in Clarence, New York.

Bill's service in the military had a great impact on his life. Bill was a gunner in an airplane squadron during World War II. During those years, he saw the world and experienced a coming of age. He learned the harsh reality of life and death, after witnessing a third of his companions lose their lives. When the war ended, Bill returned home a changed man, determined never again to take life, and its opportunities, for granted. At the age of twenty-five, Bill decided to start college, entering Cornell University on a G.I. Bill scholarship, and eventually attaining a bachelors degree in electrical engineering. He attributes much of his later success to the foundation he established at Cornell, and takes pride in the fact that he had the courage to go back to school at a later age. He went on to complete a Masters in Electrical Engineering from the University at Buffalo.

Despite his many achievements, Bill's top priority has always been his family. Even when Bill was forced to travel frequently for business, he never spent weekends away from home. He has been married to his wife Eleanor for almost sixty years and they have raised five children together. Although they have accumulated wealth, Eleanor and Bill have lived a humble life, remaining in the same simple farmhouse for over forty years.

Over the years, Eleanor and Bill have given away much of their money to the church, the community, education, and numerous other social causes. In their area, they have a reputation for utmost generosity. If someone asks for help, and it's a worthy cause, Eleanor and Bill will frequently contribute. As an example of his extraordinary kindness, Bill pays for the education of all of his employees and all of his employees' children. The Greatbatch's strong Christian faith has guided them throughout their life.

I met with Wilson at Greatbatch Enterprises in Clarence, New York:

Q: At what point did you start believing that you were meant for something great?

A: I guess I never put much in that. I still regard myself as one of the Lord's little people.

Q: In the early days of your research, did you conceive of the impact that your work would eventually have?

A: I don't think so. We were driven by curiosity. Money never really entered into it at all. It's a good thing because the whole pacemaker project started out with $2000 in cash and enough to feed my family for two years. I gave my money to my wife. I quit all my jobs much to her consternation and went out to the barn behind my house. In two years, I built fifty pacemakers out there. Who could have visualized a ten billion dollar industry?

Q: How did you come up with your revolutionary ideas?

A: I think it was basically curiosity. Why does it work and what makes it work? Can we make it work better? Input for our ideas largely comes from talking to people.

Q: But when you have the actual idea, is it an epiphany?

A: Even now, I find that my best ideas come at four o' clock in the morning. A lot of the ideas never work out. Nine things out of ten never work.

Q: At four o' clock in the morning, are you inspired by your dreams? Is there a value to being a dreamer in life?

A: It removes the limitations on your thinking. You need to expand your horizons. You can't afford to limit them.

Q: What else does it take to be an inventor or revolutionary thinker?

A: You're not going to make it looking to be a financial success. Most of the things are not financial successes. I don't look at the costs and the economics. If you come up with a real solution to a real problem, don't worry about what it costs.

Q: How important is it to have confidence in yourself, in being an inventor and, more generally, in being successful?

A: I think it's very important. On the other hand, it's also very important to recognize your own limitations. There are a lot of things that would be nice to have, but they're just not possible. I've known people that have spent their whole career barking away at some medical problem and never get a solution to it. I think one of my strengths is knowing when to say, "Well, I've really given it my best, but it's not working—it's time to move on to something else."

Q: Would you say you're as passionate today as you were when you first started?

A: Oh yes, I want to go forward with this. I figure that I have three hundred and nineteen patents now, and I have twenty more pending. I figure that when I get up to about four hundred, one of my patents will be longevity. [Laughing] Our mission statement shows where we'll be fifty years from now. Normally, I'd be dead by then, but who knows. [Laughing]

Q: Obviously, work makes you happy. Would you have been as happy with your work if your inventions had not been so successful?

A: If nothing that I did ever worked, then I probably wouldn't be (happy). The fact that I can get ten percent success is enough.

People get upset over success and failure. I don't think that the good Lord really cares about whether you succeed or whether you fail. He wants you to try and try hard, and that's all that is required of you. So I'll never shoot myself over failure or never look with exalt over success. I really don't care. I do care that I try and I try hard.

Q: Do you handle failure well, because you don't view it as failure?

A: It's not failure—it is a learning experience. As I said before, the person who has never failed is probably the person who has never done anything.

Q: Does it take failing many times in order to be able to succeed in your life?

A: That's what Edison said. They said, "Well, you tried a thousand things for that light bulb. Isn't it time you gave up?" He replied, "No, now I know a thousand things I'm not going to try." [Laughing] He was my hero really. I think all the things that drove him, drove me—curiosity, business. He liked the business side of it; he did pretty well.

Q: In the early development of the pacemaker, you left everything to pursue this invention. How were you able to take such a risk?

A: If we didn't do it, it would never get done. We knew we could do it, and we didn't think anyone else could do it. I never thought of it as a risk, just something I had to do.

Q: You just had that much confidence in yourself at that point?

A: Well, I didn't care. I was curious. I guess part of it is almost a religious view. If I know what I should do and it's a good thing in the Lord's sight, then something will happen. Maybe this won't work, but it will lead to something that will.

Q: You seem to follow your gut feelings instead of allowing the outside world to dictate your actions?

A: Absolutely. In fact, I ignore the outside world. If I let the outside world guide me, I wouldn't be running this business.

Q: How big of a role does fate play in what you have done in life?

A: I've heard it said that serendipity favors the prepared mind.

Q: So let's talk a little bit about your life influences. Growing up in the Depression generation, did your family struggle financially?

A: We didn't know it, but we were really poor.

Q: How did this affect you?

A: I think it made me more self-reliant because I had to go to work and help my father.

Q: After years of helping your father, you entered the military to fight in World War II. What did you learn from serving in the military?

A: I learned how to manage people. I was head man in the squadron and was in charge of all the gunners.

Q: So then you came back after the service, and entered Cornell. How old were you when you first entered college?

A: I was about twenty-five. I was in the Navy for five years. People said, well, you lost five years—how will you ever catch up? In the first five years out of college, I caught up with a lot of them.

Q: What would you tell people about the importance of education in their lives?

A: Anything you learn is going to help you.

Q: I guess that's part of the reason that you offer to pay for all the education of your employees and the education of their children.

A: That's one of the things that differentiates us from everybody else, and one of the things that has paid off most for us.

Q: So getting back to more your personal philosophy, what is the biggest reason that you believe that you've become so successful?

A: I think the reason would be that we look at everything that we do from another person's point of view. We find out what the weak points of the device are, and then we go back home and fix it. Not too many companies do that these days.

Q: How have you been able to overcome adversity in your life?

A: It's the ability to put things in their proper context. It's realizing the things that are important and the things that are not. Adversity is always a challenge I guess, but it's a good challenge. Overcoming difficult things is a good feeling.

Q: It makes you stronger?

A: Stronger and smarter.

Q: How would you advise other people to become successful in their lives?

A: I'd say don't think about it. I'd say make sure you're interested in what you're doing. If you're not, you better find something else to do. Also, don't mind working hard—put your whole heart and soul into what you're doing.

Q: What's the secret to being happy and being fulfilled in your life?

A: Well, it's recognizing the difference between success and failure—the meaninglessness of the difference between success and failure. Also, I believe that the teachings of the ages—whether it be Hinduism or Buddhism or the Koran or the Jewish Old Testament or the Christian New Testament or the Chinese Confucian teachings—all of them are very useful. They all lead to the same thing, which is a minimization of the materialistic aspect of life. It's very important. It takes all the stress out of living.

Q: How important is teamwork and the ability to work with other people in becoming successful?

A: So important. You never do anything by yourself. It's always teamwork. Very few people do a lot by themselves.

Q: In your opinion, what are the key elements of good teamwork?

A: Listening. Same as raising a family, it's ninety percent listening. If I get ten percent of the airtime, it's pretty dramatic. You have to listen.

Q: What has your family meant to you in your life?

A: Family is everything. It was the first priority, even when I was starting the companies. I never spent a weekend away from home.

Q: Having done all the things you have done, if you did not have a family, would it have been as fulfilling?

A: It would be pretty meaningless. I couldn't imagine that.

Q: How about God? You keep mentioning Him in our conversation. What role has God played in your life?

A: Well, I can't tell other people that they have to believe in God; that has to come from them. I can say that in my own life, it has been a determining factor. He guided my life, and He lent me strength, mental and physical, to accomplish the things that I wanted to do.

Q: What has motivated you in your life? Has it been glory, other people, family, yourself, God?

A: Well, a little bit of everything, but primarily the Lord. Knowing what He wants me to do and striving to do things that will make this a better world for Him.

Q: What's the most important thing that you've learned over your lifetime?

A: I think first Corinthians 10:24—the other person's welfare is always more important than your own.

Q: What is the meaning of life?

A: I guess to do the Lord's work. I think I have an obligation on me to utilize what the good Lord has given me. In fact, every decision I make really, whether it's for work or family, I ask myself if this is a good thing in the Lord's sight. If it is, we go ahead. If it's not, why waste our time? We stop and do something different.

Q: What has given you the greatest satisfaction in your life?

A: I guess just the opportunity to do the things that I do—to build these things and see them used, and to build a company around some really amazing people.

Q: You feel a responsibility for people who work here?

A: Oh yes, definitely.

Q: Do you have any regrets in life?

A: I regret that I didn't spend more time with my family than I did. I passed a lot of time working. Yet (if I hadn't), I may not have finished what I was working on. There is always give and take, but basically the answer is no.

Bill feels an enormous sense of responsibility—to his family, to society and to God. His responsibility, and ultimately his success, are based on the inherent conviction that the other person's welfare is always more important than his own. Bill believes that his natural skills and talents are a divine gift, and he therefore has a duty to utilize what has been given to him to glorify God. In everything Bill does, he seeks to be an ethical person, assist those in need, lead by example, and positively impact the world.

At Greatbatch Enterprises, everyone was genuinely friendly. They're the kind of people who make a stranger feel right at home, by exchanging a few caring words or offering to lend a needed hand. It is difficult to find employees who are happier, kinder and more devoted to, and proud of, their organization. When they heard I was writing a book, they wanted to make sure that the world knew that their boss was one of the most extraordinary people in the world. With heartfelt emotion, they shared wonderful stories about their lives, describing how they lived in the same neighborhoods, went to the same church, and even sang in the choir together. How refreshing it was to see such camaraderie and loyalty among people who have a sense of responsibility and love for one another. They were a community, a family. They were a vision of a better, truer life.

We live in a society where few individuals are willing to accept responsibility for their actions. People are always looking to blame someone else. Too often we disregard honesty and ethics in pursuit of selfish gain. Over time, this attitude inevitably leads to loneliness, distrust and a feeling of meaninglessness. However, witnessing the life of Wilson Greatbatch makes the cynicism that is so prevalent in our society seem foolish and false. His example teaches us that social contribution leads to a stronger sense of community, as well as personal achievement and a feeling of higher purpose—all of the things we gain from living life the right way. It all comes down to assuming responsibility—taking care of one another, making a difference, and just being a good, decent human being. Wilson Greatbatch shows us that a better world is possible. We just all have to be willing to do our part to get it!

—CHAPTER 19—

MANIFEST DESTINY

MEL KLEIN

What role does fate play in our lives? Do we make our own destinies or are things just meant to be?

Mel Klein is a highly acclaimed Wall Street fund manager and financier. Although he is not well known to the public, there are few heavy-hitters in America that don't know about Mel's business clout. Running GKH Investments, a $550 million venture capital partnership, with a lot of his own money, he has averaged astounding returns over fifteen years. His other two partners have been Dan Lufkin, originally of Donaldson, Lufkin & Jenrette, and the Pritzker family, the billionaire owners of the Hyatt Hotel empire. Over the years, these three partners have bought, restructured and managed enormous companies such as American Medical International (Tenet Healthcare), Hanover Compressor, Santa Fe Energy (Devon Energy) and Savoy Pictures (USA Interactive). In Hollywood, Mel's successful ventures have produced such films as *Sophie's Choice*, *Shadowlands*, *Bronx Tale*, and *The Fugitive*.

Before starting his career in high finance, Mel earned a law degree from Columbia University and served as the director of special research in Vice President Hubert Humphrey's presidential campaign. However, it was during his undergraduate days at Colgate University that Mel learned his most valuable lesson about life. Late one night, Mel and two of his closest friends were driving home in a convertible, after a night of socializing and drinking at a party. Mel's friends sat in the front, while Mel sat dangerously on the back hood, with only his feet holding him in the automobile. As the driver took a sudden, sharp turn, Mel was thrown from the car. Only moments later, he heard a horrible crash and loud explosion. In shock from the ordeal, Mel would soon learn that both of his friends had been instantaneously killed. Many times after that night, Mel asked himself why he was spared. He came to conclude that fate saved him for some special reason. From that day forward, he promised himself to cherish every single moment, and never again take life for granted. He wanted to work even harder than before so that he could fulfill his dreams. In no small way, that fateful car accident played a role in making Mel the overwhelming success he is today.

Mel has been married to his wife Annette for almost thirty years, and together they have raised two daughters. Until recently, Mel and Annette have made their primary residence in Corpus Christi, Texas in order to give their daughters a small-town, value-oriented upbringing. Mel has had to travel frequently in order to manage his business dealings all over the world. Yet, somehow he also has found time to be an adjunct professor at Texas A&M and a popular newspaper columnist for the *Corpus Christi Caller-Times*. Throughout his life, Mel has strongly believed in social responsibility; he is a committed philanthropist who especially cares about medical research, education and assisting the poor.

I met with Mel at his GKH Partners office in Chicago, Illinois:

Q: Was there one characteristic that made you very successful?

A: Dan Lufkin was interviewed years later, and he was asked why I was the one person that, after he had left DLJ, really became a partner of his throughout much of his career. He commented with respect to my perseverance and most importantly of all, when I had a responsibility, I always got it done. I never had excuses.

Q: Would you say those principles help you achieve great things, not only in business but in life?

A: Yes, ultimately the really critical characteristics begin with curiosity, where you're continually learning. Growing and learning help build your judgment, and judgment is the major differentiating factor among people. I would say judgment, perseverance, never quitting, a good value system, passion and a commitment that directs and empowers you.

Q: Did you have to work to find the career you loved, or was it serendipity?

A: I'm sure there's an aspect of both. I certainly was very focused on it. And I certainly had an objective of really being in business with the leading people in the country, if not the world. I think I was fortunate enough to do that. I mean, my partners for thirty years were Dan Lufkin, Jay Pritzker and Tom Pritzker. The *Wall Street Journal* named Dan Lufkin one of the hundred people who were most influential in finance in the world in the twentieth century. And probably the summary on Jay Pritzker would be that Warren Buffet once wrote in his letter to Berkshire Hathaway investors that the smartest investor that he had known was Jay Pritzker. I think my partners are extraordinary people, very bright, very principled. I was privileged to be very close to them as friends and as business partners for many years.

Q: That's definitely an essential characteristic, to surround yourself with the right environment, with the right people?

A: Essential.

Q: What does it take to be a visionary?

A: I think it takes constant learning and reading, trying to stay aware of what is going on, enhancing your knowledge base. I've always found it has been a combination of a lot of perspiration, a lot of study, a lot of hard work that precedes the inspiration. The inspiration doesn't just come out of a bolt of lightning.

Q: What is the significance of making mistakes along the way?

A: You learn from them. You grow from them. And certainly, living through adversity makes you much stronger. After time, it gives you a sense of understanding of what can happen in life. Perspective is very important.

Q: How about your ability to take risks?

A: Well, basically we're all at risk. I mean, from the moment we're born to the time that we die, we're at risk. But you need to assume risk and take risk in a conscientious way to ever advance yourself. Without risk, there's no advancement.

Q: Do you need an ability to accept failure?

A: Yes, you need to be able to accept failure and accept that you're not perfect. You need to have a certain clear, fundamental humility about yourself and about life. I think that's essential to being a good human being as well as a good businessperson.

Q: As a successful businessman and entrepreneur, how are you able to balance work with family?

A: Imperfectly. There are certainly periods of time, where if you could do it over again, you'd balance it differently. So it's a constant balancing. Everything is balancing. You're making trade-offs all the time. Judgment is the key variable. Make choices.

Make judgments. And only in retrospect, will you know whether you made the right one.

Q: You grew up in a modest background. Your parents were both working class. What kind of impact did that have on you?

A: I come from a very warm and loving family. And the support that I got from my parents was invaluable. The fact that I grew up in modest financial circumstances really motivated me to become financially successful.

Q: It made you work harder?

A: It made me work very hard. I was determined to be successful, and would not accept any other alternative other than success.

Q: Growing up, who were the people that had the greatest impact on you?

A: Certainly my parents, and my maternal grandparents especially. Just wonderful people—loving, warm, really good values. Then of course people I read about. I've been a prodigious reader my whole life. I've been a lifelong student.

Q: You like reading nonfiction and biographies?

A: Yes, I like reading about the real world accomplishments, successes and contributions of people.

Q: Were there any events while you were growing up that really changed you?

A: Certainly. One experience that I had my freshman year in college did change my life. Parents weekend of my freshman year I was the only survivor of a drunk-driving accident that I was in with two of my fraternity brothers.

Q: Did that experience make you value your life more?

A: It really did. That experience changed my life in a number of ways. I have not ever had a drink of hard liquor since that night. And it made me view life very differently, a lot more responsibly. I've always felt that there had to be some purpose or some reason that I was spared that evening.

Q: What would you tell other people who don't appreciate the opportunities they are given in life?

A: Seize them. You have one life to lead and if you don't lead it, it's your loss and your tragedy. And you really need to make the most out of all the time that you have, because you just don't know what can happen in life.

Q: Can you talk a little bit about the meaning of education in your life and how important it is in general?

A: I think part of the purpose of life is to educate yourself throughout your entire life. Education is not something you take only at one point in your life. Curiosities, the habits of learning, stay with you through your entire life.

Q: What has family meant to you over the years?

A: I treasure my family. I treasure close friendships. I just think they're invaluable and an absolutely essential part of life's journey to make it worthwhile.

Q: Would the business successes you've had mean as much if you didn't have your family?

A: Absolutely not. Family and friendship mean far more.

Q: You've been involved in quite a number of social causes. What does that stem from? Is it a social responsibility?

A: Yes, and I think we all have a responsibility to others. Unless individuals have a sense of responsibility to others in their community, we can't sustain this extraordinary country. Individual people have to do their respective part in making that which they come in touch with better.

Q: Would you say you've felt a pressure to achieve great things in your life? Have you set a very high standard for yourself?

A: Yes, I've always felt a burning desire and commitment to continually achieve, grow and keep moving forward.

Q: What has given you the greatest satisfaction?

A: Seeing people that I love happy, healthy.

Q: Throughout your life, what are the greatest things you've learned from your experiences?

A: How much more there is to always learn. Try to be understanding of other people's circumstances and don't be judgmental. Try to understand where other people are coming from. There's a lot of adversity, and a lot of people are afflicted with issues that are very challenging for them. I think it's important to be supportive. I think it's important to do all you can to alleviate the pain of others. Try to make it a better world.

Q: What do you believe is the meaning of life?

A: Try to understand yourself. Try to understand how you fit into the universe, history and the scheme of things. And try to positively advance that with which you come in meaningful contact.

Q: How essential is self-awareness?

A: Very essential. The unexamined life isn't worth living.

Q: Do you have to be honest with yourself?

A: Very honest. I think much of the purpose of life is to achieve a greater and greater level of self-understanding, self-honesty. You can't really get some place where you'd like to go until you understand where you've been, where you are, who you are, and why you are who you are.

Q: How about when you're young, how do you make those decisions?

A: I think you want to explore broadly. I think you want to explore a lot of alternatives. So many people go into areas for reasons they don't understand. I think when you're younger, you want to advance yourself in every way you can. You want to grow. You want to learn. You want to explore. The key is to be open. You want to be open to ideas. You want to be open to alternatives. And then after you've done a lot of exploring and learning and living and feeling and growing—there will be a time to make choices.

Q: In your own life, would you say you're more prone to follow your heart or your mind?

A: My heart.

Q: You initially go with the instinct?

A: Follow your passion.

Q: How do you take an idea and make it manifest into reality?

A: The first thing you need to do is think about what are the key variables necessary to actualizing the idea. Then you need to marshal those resources. Direct them, guide them, pull them together, use them as you need to and then provide the energy source and the perseverance to actualize them. That's what it's about. It's not just thinking about it. It's not just making excuses about why it doesn't happen. It's not just rationalizing. If you have an idea that you want brought to fruition, you need to envision it being realized.

Q: Once you have a job you stick with it until it's completed?

A: Yes. I think it's a very, very significant differentiator among people. Most people on this planet really don't know what they want. They kind of have some vague ideas. So if you don't know what you want, it's hard to get it. Then other people know what they want or think they know what they want, but they don't know how to get it and are not prepared to do what is necessary to get it.

Q: What does integrity mean to you?

A: It means a lot. It is involved in how you treat your neighbor, your friends, your family and the average person with whom you come in contact. It means doing what is right, because it is right.

Q: How do you reconcile seeing very successful people who lack integrity?

A: It's sad. A lot of people take short cuts. A lot of people try to get to places no matter what standards they follow. I believe it's important to get to as high a place as you can, following higher standards.

Q: Is there value in being a dreamer?

A: Yes, being a dreamer combined with an action-orientation is a tremendous combination. Without dreams, you don't have progress or change.

Q: Do you think as a leader you have a responsibility to act in a certain way?

A: Absolutely, you have a responsibility to look after the best interests of the people.

Q: Do you think some people in our society have dropped the ball in terms of being good leaders?

A: Well, I think there are a lot of people that are celebrities. I think you have to define leaders and differentiate leaders and celebrities. There are people that are strictly media creations. You know, Donald Trump has developed a brand based upon self-promotion. There are a lot of people that are self-promoters. I wouldn't call them leaders. I would just say they're celebrities and the press has become sloppy and failed to define true, capable, worthy leaders as such.

Q: So what's the secret to living a happy and fulfilled life?

A: I'd like to find that out. [Laughing] Maybe I'll do that when I read your book. [Laughing]

Q: I can't promise anything. [Laughing] Would you say society's values have changed during the course of your lifetime?

A: Absolutely, primarily related to what we just talked about, the omni-present aspect of media.

Q: What kind of effect is that having on society?

A: I think it has created a need for a skill of information selection. There's such a proliferation of information. There's so much media creation of celebrities. Real leaders and people truly worthy of that admiration are not necessarily those that are in the spotlight all the time. They're more concerned with their accomplishments; more concerned with doing good than they are with touting it. And so I think there is a growing gap between image and reality.

Q: In society, are people not taking responsibility for their own actions?

A: Not only are they not taking responsibility for their own actions, they're looking for the easy street—without work and effort. They're looking to hit the jackpot.

Q: Do you think there should be responsibility on the part of mass media?

A: I do. You know, there are two answers to that. Some people say, well it's the market. If there's no demand for it, there wouldn't be a product. But I think sometimes the product stimulates the demand. I think there should be standards. I think there's a certain responsibility that goes with control of that which influences a large number of people.

Q: Do you think we've grown more or less connected as a society?

A: Previously, if you wanted to chat, you would go to your neighbor's porch and you would chat in person. Now you've got chat rooms where there are a lot of connections, but it's impersonal. You don't see the people. I think we're less connected personally.

Q: If you had the power to change one thing in the world, what would that be?

A: I'd make more brunettes, blonde. [Laughing] Certainly, you want to bring about peace in the world. You want to remove the causes of terror, discrimination and thoughtlessness. You want to remove that what makes small children cry. You want to take the pain away. Relieve the suffering—there's a lot of suffering in the world. You want to help people and make their lives better.

What's most interesting about Mel is his belief that fate holds a greater purpose. When his life was spared in the car accident, he concluded that it was saved for a reason. This experience crystallized his value system, increased his appreciation for living, and made him even more ambitious. Mel went on to become an accomplished scholar, admired professor, acclaimed writer, devoted philanthropist, revered business leader and loved family man. Behind this extraordinary success, has been the underlying conviction that he is meant to do what he is doing for a greater reason. Through this belief in the power of fate, Mel creates his own self-fulfilling prophecy.

Beyond the unforeseeable events, such as accidents, sickness and death, everyone has control over their own destiny. Most of the time, the most difficult part is simply figuring out what you want in your life. Once you know what you want, and you start taking the necessary steps to get it, it's just a matter of time until you achieve your goals. In Mel's case, a near death experience was a catalyst that prompted him to focus on what he wanted out of life, and to do what it took to get it. Would he have reached the same conclusions about life without that experience? Who knows? His working-class upbringing had left him with the ambition to achieve great success in life. He was smart, confident, curious and hard-working. However, that fateful car accident may have been the final link that brought it all together.

Our experiences do define us, but the fact is that each one of us has control over the decisions that we make. Who do you want to be? Where do you want to go? How do you want to live? As beneficiaries of the American Dream, we live in a country where all of these questions are open-ended. Each one of us has the final say. For better or worse, most of us will not have a fateful, near-death experience like Mel Klein. However, we all share one common denominator. We will all eventually die. It's a harsh reality, but it's true. With that in mind, all of life becomes essentially a near-death experience. So why not make the best of our limited time? By discovering what we truly want, and believing in fate, we create our own self-fulfilling prophecies. Live to the fullest of your ability, and you will determine your own destiny!

—Chapter 20—

Humility

Colleen Barrett

Do you think you're better than everyone else? Do you know your weaknesses and limitations? Can humility be your greatest strength?

Colleen Barrett is currently the president and chief operations officer of Southwest Airlines, but she did not begin her career at the top. Coming from a humble background, with no money or connections, she earned a trade degree and became a legal secretary. Colleen worked as a secretary for many years, and did not aspire to be anything greater. But through her consistent work ethic and charming personality, she gradually rose through the ranks, until she became one of the most influential women in America. Although she has become extremely successful, Colleen has not changed as a person. To this day, she is known for her kindness, humility, and simple, everyday demeanor. The same qualities that attracted people to Colleen when she was a secretary have helped make her an effective, and respected leader. Like many of the subjects in this book, Colleen is a champion to the common person, because her path in life truly shows that anything is possible.

Colleen began her career as an assistant for Herb Kelleher, the present-day chairman of Southwest Airlines. Forty years later, they are still working side-by-side, and their complementary personalities have formed an amazing business partnership. Colleen's break came more than ten years after she started as Herb's assistant, when she was asked to organize Southwest's Customer Relations Department. At the time, the department only had two employees, and Colleen did not see it as a huge opportunity. Without worrying about where it might lead, she decided to put everything she had into her responsibilities, and the rest was history. Her work created many of Southwest's Golden Rules for treatment of customers, and ultimately resulted in the airline's winning culture. Over time, her loving, nurturing personality became a trademark for the company. In large part, Colleen's efforts have helped make Southwest the largest, most profitable business in the airline industry.

Colleen has a son, Patrick, who she raised on her own after divorcing quite young. Patrick now has his own family, with a wife and son, Evan, who is Colleen's pride and joy. In addition to her real family, Southwest Airlines has truly become Colleen's extended family over the years. She personally writes birthday and employment anniversary cards to many of the employees, and is generally considered the surrogate mother of the Southwest organization.

In her personality and appearance, Colleen is one-of-a-kind. The day of our interview, she wore a casual summer outfit of white pants and a loose-fitting shirt, with colorful, glittery, heart-shaped designs, that matched the designs on her socks. A pair of comfortable tennis shoes completed the ensemble. Her long gray hair was pulled back in a ponytail, showing off her round, expressive face, and caring eyes. Her manner exuded warmth, politeness and humility. During our time together, it seemed amazing to me that this pleasant, soft-spoken lady was one of the most powerful businesspeople in the country. She reminded me more of my loving mother than a corporate giant, and I kept waiting for her to offer me some apple pie.

I met with Colleen at Southwest Airlines corporate headquarters in Dallas, Texas:

Q: You've achieved so much in your life. Would you have ever expected that you would be here today?

A: Absolutely not, really and truly. I think probably, to the extent that I have been successful, it is because I had no career path. Today, everyone talks about servant leadership, but I think I was just sort of born to be a servant leader. I get my highs and my best satisfactions when I feel that I have solved a problem or I have helped to make a situation better. I don't do it for pay; I don't do it for recognition or reward. I do it because it makes me feel good.

Q: What's your secret? How did you advance from essentially a secretarial position, to become president of a large company?

A: In a nutshell, I think I had a customer service orientation from the get-go. Even when I was a legal secretary, my strengths were that I was a fairly good listener and someone that people would automatically come to talk to. Even at the law firm, I sort of became the voice of the non-legal staff. It evolved; it wasn't a planned thing. I also loved to write—I started drafting a lot of the responses to customer letters, shareholder letters and employee letters. So I was right in the middle of it all. That is really how I learned the operations. Eventually, I set up the first real customer relations department.

Q: So the customer relations department was your first official switch?

A: Yes, and I did it for a couple of years, really as Herb's assistant more than anything else. But over time, I literally set up the system that we still use today.

Q: When you were starting off in your career, what were your intentions and goals?

A: I just wanted to do whatever Herb needed done. It was as simple as that.

Q: You obviously love what you do. How do you find the kind of work that you love, is it something that you have to look for or is serendipity involved?

A: I have a personal philosophy, and I share it quite often with people. Never take a job for the pay or the title. I just wouldn't and couldn't do a job that I didn't enjoy. Life is just too short. [Laughing]

Q: I think a lot of people need to hear that.

A: Yes. I encourage people quite frequently to change direction. Sometimes you have to take a step down in order to take a step up.

Q: So is that what you would advise a person if they asked you how to become successful in their lives?

A: I guess if someone said to me, "What do I need to do to be successful?" I would have to say, "Well, what are your passions and what are your values and what are your goals and how do you want to lead your life? Once you decide that then do it with purpose, passion and vision."

Q: Do you feel like you have a greater purpose behind what you do?

A: [Laughing] Well, I don't know. Southwest has been the culture. We've sort of been referred to as being cultish. [Laughing] I'm very proud of this fact. This is not propaganda; this is not advertising or PR. I want employees to feel when they join Southwest, that they're joining a cause. We can literally make a difference, a positive difference, everyday, individually. People are empowered to make those altruistic, warm, and caring gestures to each other.

Q: You personally write birthday and anniversary cards. I guess it is part of that Southwest culture, but it also seems to be your personal passion. Why?

A: I don't know. I'm just an Irish sentimental slob. [Laughing] We said from day one, that we wanted our employees to feel like they were a family. We really meant that.

Q: Does it give you a sense of responsibility to take care of the people?

A: Oh yes, what a burden. [Laughing] I think most people would affectionately say that I'm sort of thought of as one of the parents. [Laughing] Sometimes that might not be said as affectionately as others, but I really do think of this as my family. I think of all of these people as being my kids, no matter how old. It's a huge responsibility.

Q: You really take care of the Southwest employees. Like a good mother, it seems like you encourage everyone to be themselves?

A: If you have to be someone other than yourself, then you aren't truly contributing your part to whatever it is that you're trying to do. I can't imagine anything worse than that. It's one of the things that I spend a lot of time talking to our employees about. If you come into our organization with a mindset that you are supposed to fill a mold in your job, please leave that at the door, because we don't want molds. [Laughing] We don't want robots. We don't want people to look alike, talk alike and dress alike. We hire you because of your individuality. We hire you because something about you in your interview told us that you're a perfect fit attitude-wise.

Q: You're such a positive person. Tell me about your background. Did you grow up in a smaller town?

A: Yes, itty bitty. [Laughing] Bellows Falls, Vermont.

Q: Did your family struggle financially?

A: We were a very poor family, as almost everyone in Vermont is.

[Laughing] Pretty humble beginnings—I don't think either of my parents had any formal education beyond high school. My dad went to the Navy right out of school. My mother was a laborer; she was a keypunch operator at a dye company, and worked six days a week for many, many years. She raised three kids—I have two brothers. My dad worked at the post office, when he worked. He was an alcoholic and really didn't contribute a lot to the family. You kind of just knew from the get-go, that you have to work hard for a good day's pay.

Q: Did you pay your own way through school?

A: I did. I got one of those government loans that I paid off for ten years. I lived on five dollars a week; I did a lot of babysitting.

Q: Who were the people that made the greatest impression on you during your childhood?

A: I had teachers that had a great influence on me. I went to Catholic school through the eighth grade, and I had one nun who took a special interest in me. Even today, I still quote the dear lady—Sister Mary Thomas. Also, in high school, I had an English teacher for four years named Richard Jillson. I was scared to death of him. I think the nun taught me the basics, pounded them into me. Not only values but the basics of math, English, etc. I think that Mr. Jillson pounded into me to write and have a decent vocabulary. I'm kind of a slow learner, really an over-achiever. I'll plug and plug away, but learning doesn't come easily. I'm not a genius. I mean, I'm far from an intellectual. Mr. Jillson just taught me the value of being good at what you're doing, and he really challenged me.

Q: Getting back to some of your personal philosophies, what were some of the challenges that you've had to overcome?

A: The only thing that I can think of is more of a social thing. I had a few embarrassing moments when I went to a couple political fund-raisers. Some people made you feel like, "Who are you and what are you doing here?"

Q: How did that affect you?

A: Well, I don't know. My mother always just embedded in me, that no one was better than I was, and I wasn't better than anyone. I guess I'm self-confident. I don't think I'm cocky. I kind of know who I am. I know my strengths and weaknesses. I know when I am in over my head, versus when I am not.

Q: Well, I'm sure you'll have no problems with that, walking into a room now.

A: Yes. [Laughing]

Q: How are you able to get over the mistakes that you make?

A: By seeking forgiveness, acknowledging the mistakes and trying to correct them. I think you grow and learn from every mistake that you make. And some are more serious than others, but you have to just kind of confess. [Laughing] As a Catholic, you know, it's kind of like going to confession. [Laughing]

Q: How important is attitude?

A: We put in our ads that we hire for attitude, train for skills. Don't get nervous, we don't hire pilots that can't fly airplanes. [Laughing] I think attitude is everything.

Q: How do you balance your work with your personal life?

A: I'm probably not a role model in that regard. Although I wouldn't say my work habits destroyed my marriage or anything like that. But, I will say, I decided very quickly after I got divorced that I couldn't be all things to all people. I could only balance so much. Within a year of my divorce, maybe two, I pretty much decided I could be a great secretary. I could be a good mom. But I couldn't have yet a third hat. Dating—I just couldn't do it. I was going to have quality time with Patrick; I was going to make sure that I wasn't going to miss anything that was important to him.

Between that and my job, that was going to fill seven days a week. That's a conscious decision that I made. I don't know; you'd have to ask him. I think I did okay. [Laughing]

Q: How did you balance your work with being a good mother?

A: I think you just have to set your priorities, and I think you need to express to your family why work is also important for the overall picture. I encourage my guys to bring their kids to work once in awhile. I think it's important, and I always did this with Patrick when he was small. You have to work, but there is a way to balance all that.

Q: Work has definitely been a major part of your life?

A: Oh yes, it is my life. [Laughing] But that's a conscious choice too. People need to consciously think about what they want in terms of balance in their own life.

Q: What would you say has motivated you most in your life?

A: I think a sense of accomplishment—a self-test. Almost everyday before I go to sleep I will ask, did I have a good day? Did I get something decent done today? Did I accomplish something?

Q: This self-test sounds like a tool that promotes self-awareness. How essential is self-awareness to you?

A: Oh, very. If you don't have it, how can you even analyze the results of your day? You have to be able to recognize your strengths and your weaknesses, and I think you have to know your limitations. I think you have to know what you do well, and what you should just stay away from.

Q: Now that you mention it, what's your biggest weakness or limitation?

A: I'm not at all good at standing up and delivering a speech.

Q: Have you become more comfortable with that over the years?

A: It used to be somebody would put a guilt trip on me and I would say okay. I would go and be paralyzed. I would be awful. It just isn't who I am. So now, I just say, I don't give speeches. If you want to give me a topic, I will talk about it for ten minutes, but then I want to do forty minutes of Q & A.

Q: Despite weaknesses and limitations, do you try to see the positive in everything?

A: I try. I also just realize that you can't control things. I don't spend a lot of time crying over spilled milk.

Q: So you're an optimist—you always keep hope.

A: God, if you don't have hope, then you just have nothing. If you don't have hope, then you have despair. I don't want to live in despair. [Laughing]

Q: What's the secret to staying passionate over the years?

A: I don't know, but I think if you lose passion, life is awfully dull. [Laughing] Maybe it's just the drive to be really, really the best—doesn't really matter what it is, how big or how small. You can't do that if you don't have the passion. Maybe it's just because I really do think that life is so short for all of us. I can't imagine everyone not wanting to make the most out of everyday.

Q: What do you believe is the meaning of life?

A: To live it to the fullest. Honestly, I think to just practice the Golden Rule and to respect others.

Q: What is the Golden Rule?

A: The Golden Rule is to treat others as you would like to be treated.

Q: Is that what gives you the greatest satisfaction?

A: I like to feel like I've made a positive difference in somebody's life every day. I love doing things that touch people's hearts. I like to make people feel good about themselves—doing acts of kindness. I enjoy heart-to-heart things. I love to talk with people and get their spin on things.

Q: What's the secret to living a happy and fulfilled life?

A: I think feeling comfortable in your own skin. I think that's a very individualistic thing. Self-satisfaction, self-awareness—I'm a pretty simple person, and that's a pretty simplistic answer. [Laughing]

Q: If you over-complicate things, you just stress yourself out.

A: Yes, and you start second and third guessing yourself. It just drives me crazy when people do that.

Q: Do you believe that by being in a position of leadership, you have a responsibility to set a good example?

A: Yes, that's part of leadership—leadership by example. You cannot hold other people accountable, if you don't hold yourself accountable.

Q: If you had the power to change one thing in the world, what would it be?

A: It would be to cause all human beings to be respectful of one another. I think that's really the answer.

Q: After everything is said and done, how do you want to be remembered?

A: [Laughing] She cared.

After talking to Colleen, it's easy to understand how such a down-to-earth, nice lady could have achieved so much. Her simple, humble personality attracts people to her, builds trust, increases loyalty, and ultimately makes her an effective leader. For Colleen it's simple—follow the Golden Rule and treat each person with kindness, respect and dignity. Try your best to make a positive difference in someone's life every day. Colleen does not waste time trying to impress others, because she prefers to devote her energy to making herself a better person.

Colleen's strength comes from her ability to acknowledge her flaws, weaknesses and limitations. She openly talks about how she doesn't drive an automobile because of a depth perception problem, and she rarely uses a computer or the Internet due to her lack of comprehension for today's technology. She also admits to being a slow learner and having a difficult time making quick decisions, and speaking in public. By acknowledging her limitations with honesty and humility, Colleen knows she has nothing to be embarrassed about, and allows herself the opportunity to confront these issues and hopefully improve on them. Besides, once her supposed shortcomings are out of the way, the only thing that's left to notice is her charming personality.

Once upon a time, it was taught that *the meek shall inherit the earth. Those who are humble and seek a pure heart shall be friends with kings.* Meeting Colleen, these proverbs come to mind. It's refreshing to see that sometimes nice people really do finish first. When combined with perseverance, a strong work ethic, and many of the other qualities we've already discussed, humility makes for a truly successful life. It also is a big step in making you a good human being. What a loving world we would live in if everyone could stop trying to impress one another and display the humility, respect, understanding and kindness of Colleen Barrett.

—Chapter 21—

Conclusion

What is the meaning of life? What is the secret of happiness? It was these simple yet profound questions that set me off on the journey that became this book. I left my trading business, purchased a tape recorder, and traveled across the United States to talk with some of the most extraordinary people in the world, hoping to find answers to these questions. And now that the journey is coming to an end, the question becomes—did I find what I was looking for?

There is no doubt that I learned much about myself and the world. Each person I interviewed taught me something about life, or at the very least, refreshed my memory as to the importance of essential life principles. As I had hoped when I conceived of this project, simply being in the presence of those who had attained greatness in their lives encouraged me to strive for greatness in my own life. Throughout the process, I was undeniably inspired.

However, in all honesty, I was expecting something more. When I started on this journey, I had hoped to find something so profound that it would overwhelm me with a sense of certainty and purpose. A vision in the sky, a life-changing dream, a true mentor who would turn out to be my personal oracle—I was really looking for a sign. But as the months passed, the last of the meetings and interviews ended, and I sat down to write this book, I realized that I had yet to have such a definitive experience. For a time, this caused me much grief, and I even thought about abandoning this book. I felt like a hypocrite, asking people to follow me on a journey that led to no definite end, no conclusions.

The breakthrough finally occurred, as most do, at a time of no particular significance. I was sitting with my family at the dinner table and sharing some of my recollections from the previous year, describing my encounters with the true mentors. As I retold their stories of humor, passion and coincidence, I was suddenly struck by the epiphany I had been waiting for. I realized that the answer I was seeking would not come from any one question, any one interview, or any one individual. The answer I was seeking was hidden in the journey itself.

If this seems obvious to me now, at the time it truly felt like a revelation. While I had begun this project with a feeling of exhilaration and excitement, somewhere along the way I had become distracted by my own insecurities. Instead of moving forward, I had begun to hesitate and look inward. My vision had been clouded by self-criticism and doubt. At times during the interview process, I had felt like an imposter. Sitting on the sofa across from a Nobel Prize winner or famous philanthropist, I had thought, *who am I to be in the presence of these extraordinary individuals*? And later, when I had begun to actually write this book, I had begun to doubt my talent and abilities, *why would anyone want to read a book written by me*?

Adding to these insecurities, was the unexpected sense of obligation I felt. Not only would the book have to satisfy me, but it would have to be worthy of my subjects. It would have to represent the people I had met in a just and honorable way and bring their wonderful stories to the world. Many nights I lost sleep, fearing that I did not have the talent or ability to handle such a task. I felt as if I had jumped into unknown waters and was now in over my head, struggling to find my bearings. At times I even reminisced of how nice and calm my life had been as a financial markets trader. Sure, I had felt that my actions were meaningless, but at least I was familiar with what was required of me. My new path, on the other hand, was uncertain and unchartered—I was frightened to death.

It was only during that dinner table conversation with my family, as I recalled my encounters with the true mentors, that my doubts vanished and the meaning of the project became clear. I had done it! I had changed my life. I had met some of the most extraordinary people in our world today, and was on the verge of completing the book that I had envisioned. All of the things that I had dreamed of were becoming a reality. However, more important than the sense of achievement, was the realization that this experience had become a part of me. For the rest of my life, I will carry with me what I have done, in my memories and in my heart.

That was my revelation. Whatever the fate of this book, it is now and forever a part of me. It is my proof that each of us can take our dreams and bring them into the world. It is a story that I can tell and be proud of for the rest of my days, a story that my grandchildren will one day know. As a financial markets trader, I was succeeding in life by most standards. I could have continued to live in that fashion, and ignored the questions that were keeping me awake at night. Instead, I decided to follow my dream. And in doing so I saw a glimpse of the truth, a hint to the answers I had been seeking. The meaning of life, and the secret to happiness, are one and the same—live your life to the fullest. Do everything that you can to make your dreams become a reality. Bring something of your own into this world. Do your best to have a positive impact on those around you. Treasure existence and cherish every moment.

Our lives are created by each of us. Reality is but a dream, manifested through persistence and conviction. As many of us know, the truth is often unimaginable, stranger than any fictional novel. The greatest accomplishments of man, be they for good or bad, all begin with a single idea. Before they were accomplished, who would have dreamed of a man on the moon, an airplane that flies the speed of sound, or a pacemaker for the human heart? Who would have imagined the horrors of the modern world, such as genocide or nuclear holocaust? For better or for worse, each of us has the power to shape the future of the world.

We live in but a flashing moment of time. We are given a century if we're lucky, and then we're gone—off to a place we can only imagine. Even a hundred years is nothing compared to how long the earth has been around, and how long it will continue once we have left it behind. No matter how much we accomplish in our lives, there will come a time when the world will not remember our names. Even the rarest of individuals can only hope to be remembered for a few centuries.

What we have is right now. What we have is this moment, and the power to shape it however we choose. There are so many things that we can decide to do with this moment. And life is but an accumulation of various moments, and various choices. Everything we accomplish in our lives—be it making friends, falling in love, starting a family, having kids, taking risks, pursuing a goal, or following a dream—we accomplish in moments. At the end of our lives, when we reminisce and look back on our existence, it is these moments that we remember. These moments become who we are.

The meaning of life is not contained in a lightning bolt or a vision in the sky. No, the meaning of life is more tangible—it is your life, right now. It is about treating life like a precious opportunity, seizing and embracing every moment. It is about living life in such a way, that when we come to the end, we will look back without regret or fear of what's to come, for our hearts, souls and memories will already be full. We will know that we're passing on from this world, having lived a life so full, so unimaginable, that it would befit kings and queens. That will be our destiny, yours and mine, if we choose to make it thus.

—Appendix—

Here's a fun section to help you find the true mentor that is most similar to you. At the end of each interview, I gave them a test. I proposed to them a series of twenty-five questions that consisted of two words.

Take the test below, and on the following pages, see how your answers compare to the true mentors. Choose one of two words, or both, or neither:

Extrovert or Introvert?	Extrovert - Introvert - Both - Neither
Love or Money?	Love - Money - Both - Neither
Old or New?	Old - New - Both - Neither
Wisdom or Fame?	Wisdom - Fame - Both - Neither
Outside or Inside?	Outside - Inside - Both - Neither
Bungalow or Villa?	Bungalow - Villa - Both - Neither
SUV or Sports Car?	SUV – Sports Car - Both - Neither
Book or Movie?	Book - Movie - Both - Neither
Hot & Spicy or Mild?	Hot & Spicy – Mild - Both - Neither
Town or Country?	Town - Country - Both - Neither
Intelligence or Looks?	Intelligence - Looks - Both - Neither
Sprint or Stroll?	Sprint - Stroll - Both - Neither
Work or Play?	Work – Play - Both - Neither
Dreamer or Realist?	Dreamer - Realist - Both - Neither
Adventure or Romance?	Adventure - Romance - Both - Neither
Spontaneity or Routine?	Spontaneity – Routine - Both - Neither
Today or Tomorrow?	Today - Tomorrow - Both - Neither
Debater or Mediator?	Debater - Mediator - Both - Neither
Candlelight or Poker Night?	Candlelight - Poker Night - Both - Neither
Sunrise or Sunset?	Sunrise – Sunset – Both - Neither
Cluttered or Organized?	Cluttered - Organized - Both - Neither
History or Art?	History – Art – Both - Neither
Land or Sea?	Land - Sea - Both - Neither
Fiction or Nonfiction?	Fiction – Nonfiction – Both – Neither
Soup or Salad?	Soup – Salad – Both - Neither

	Steve Wozniak	Muriel Siebert	Bernie Marcus
Extrovert or Introvert	Introvert	Both	Extrovert
Love or Money	Love	Both	Love
Old or New	New	Neither	Both
Wisdom or Fame	Wisdom	Both	Wisdom
Outside or Inside	Inside	Neither	Inside
Bungalow or Villa	Bungalow	Both	Villa
SUV or Sports Car	Both	Sports Car	SUV
Book or Movie	Movie	Movie	Both
Hot & Spicy or Mild	Hot & Spicy	Both	Mild
Town or Country	Country	Both	Country
Intelligence or Looks	Intelligence	Both	Intelligence
Sprint or Stroll	Stroll	Sprint	Stroll
Work or Play	Play	Both	Both
Dreamer or Realist	Dreamer	Both	Dreamer
Adventure or Romance	Adventure	Both	Adventure
Spontaneity or Routine	Spontaneity	Spontaneity	Spontaneity
Today or Tomorrow	Today	Both	Tomorrow
Debater or Mediator	Mediator	Debater	Debater
Candlelight or Poker Night	Poker Night	Candlelight	Candlelight
Sunrise or Sunset	Sunrise	Sunset	Sunrise
Cluttered or Organized	Both	Cluttered	Cluttered
History or Art	Art	Art	History
Land or Sea	Land	Both	Land
Fiction or Nonfiction	Nonfiction	Nonfiction	Fiction
Soup or Salad	Both	Salad	Soup

	Vernon Smith	Sylvia Earle	Wally Amos
Extrovert or Introvert	Extrovert	Both	Extrovert
Love or Money	Love	Love	Love
Old or New	New	Both	Both
Wisdom or Fame	Wisdom	Wisdom	Wisdom
Outside or Inside	Outside	Both	Both
Bungalow or Villa	Bungalow	Neither	Bungalow
SUV or Sports Car	SUV	Sports Car	Neither
Book or Movie	Both	Both	Both
Hot & Spicy or Mild	Both	Hot & Spicy	Mild
Town or Country	Both	Both	Country
Intelligence or Looks	Intelligence	Intelligence	Intelligence
Sprint or Stroll	Sprint	Both	Stroll
Work or Play	Both	Both	Both
Dreamer or Realist	Dreamer	Both	Dreamer
Adventure or Romance	Adventure	Both	Both
Spontaneity or Routine	Spontaneity	Both	Spontaneity
Today or Tomorrow	Tomorrow	Both	Today
Debater or Mediator	Neither	Mediator	Mediator
Candlelight or Poker Night	Candlelight	Neither	Poker Night
Sunrise or Sunset	Both	Both	Both
Cluttered or Organized	Cluttered	Both	Organized
History or Art	Both	Both	Art
Land or Sea	Land	Sea	Both
Fiction or Nonfiction	Fiction	Both	Both
Soup or Salad	Salad	Salad	Both

	Bob Dennard	**Charito Kruvant**	**Timothy Boyle**
Extrovert or Introvert	Introvert	Both	Extrovert
Love or Money	Love	Love	Love
Old or New	Both	New	Old
Wisdom or Fame	Wisdom	Wisdom	Wisdom
Outside or Inside	Outside	Inside	Outside
Bungalow or Villa	Villa	Villa	Bungalow
SUV or Sports Car	Sports Car	SUV	Both
Book or Movie	Book	Book	Book
Hot & Spicy or Mild	Hot & Spicy	Hot & Spicy	Hot & Spicy
Town or Country	Both	Country	Both
Intelligence or Looks	Intelligence	Intelligence	Intelligence
Sprint or Stroll	Stroll	Sprint	Sprint
Work or Play	Both	Both	Both
Dreamer or Realist	Realist	Realist	Both
Adventure or Romance	Both	Adventure	Adventure
Spontaneity or Routine	Neither	Spontaneity	Spontaneity
Today or Tomorrow	Today	Today	Today
Debater or Mediator	Neither	Mediator	Debater
Candlelight or Poker Night	Candlelight	Poker Night	Candlelight
Sunrise or Sunset	Sunset	Sunrise	Sunset
Cluttered or Organized	Organized	Organized	Cluttered
History or Art	Art	Art	History
Land or Sea	Land	Land	Sea
Fiction or Nonfiction	Fiction	Nonfiction	Nonfiction
Soup or Salad	Salad	Salad	Both

	Baruch Blumberg	Raymond Damadian	Ellen Gordon
Extrovert or Introvert	Extrovert	Extrovert	Both
Love or Money	Love	Love	Both
Old or New	Both	New	Both
Wisdom or Fame	Wisdom	Wisdom	Wisdom
Outside or Inside	Both	Both	Inside
Bungalow or Villa	Villa	Bungalow	Villa
SUV or Sports Car	Neither	SUV	Sports Car
Book or Movie	Book	Book	Book
Hot & Spicy or Mild	Mild	Both	Hot & Spicy
Town or Country	Country	Country	Country
Intelligence or Looks	Intelligence	Intelligence	Intelligence
Sprint or Stroll	Stroll	Sprint	Sprint
Work or Play	Work	Work	Work
Dreamer or Realist	Both	Both	Both
Adventure or Romance	Neither	Both	Both
Spontaneity or Routine	Spontaneity	Spontaneity	Spontaneity
Today or Tomorrow	Tomorrow	Both	Tomorrow
Debater or Mediator	Mediator	Debater	Both
Candlelight or Poker Night	Poker Night	Candlelight	Candlelight
Sunrise or Sunset	Sunrise	Both	Sunrise
Cluttered or Organized	Organized	Both	Organized
History or Art	Both	History	History
Land or Sea	Land	Land	Land
Fiction or Nonfiction	Nonfiction	Nonfiction	Both
Soup or Salad	Salad	Soup	Soup

	Russell Hulse	**Delford Smith**	**James Kimsey**
Extrovert or Introvert	Introvert	Both	Extrovert
Love or Money	Love	Love	Love
Old or New	Both	Old	New
Wisdom or Fame	Wisdom	Wisdom	Wisdom
Outside or Inside	Outside	Both	Outside
Bungalow or Villa	Bungalow	Villa	Villa
SUV or Sports Car	SUV	SUV	Sports Car
Book or Movie	Book	Book	Book
Hot & Spicy or Mild	Mild	Mild	Hot & Spicy
Town or Country	Country	Country	Both
Intelligence or Looks	Intelligence	Intelligence	Intelligence
Sprint or Stroll	Stroll	Sprint	Both
Work or Play	Play	Work	Both
Dreamer or Realist	Realist	Realist	Both
Adventure or Romance	Both	Adventure	Adventure
Spontaneity or Routine	Spontaneity	Spontaneity	Spontaneity
Today or Tomorrow	Today	Both	Both
Debater or Mediator	Mediator	Mediator	Both
Candlelight or Poker Night	Candlelight	Candlelight	Candlelight
Sunrise or Sunset	Sunrise	Sunrise	Both
Cluttered or Organized	Organized	Organized	Organized
History or Art	History	History	Both
Land or Sea	Land	Neither	Land
Fiction or Nonfiction	Nonfiction	Nonfiction	Nonfiction
Soup or Salad	Soup	Both	Both

	Linda Alvarado	**Wilson Greatbatch**
Extrovert or Introvert	Both	Extrovert
Love or Money	Love	Love
Old or New	New	Both
Wisdom or Fame	Wisdom	Wisdom
Outside or Inside	Outside	Outside
Bungalow or Villa	Villa	Bungalow
SUV or Sports Car	Sports Car	SUV
Book or Movie	Book	Book
Hot & Spicy or Mild	Hot & Spicy	Mild
Town or Country	Town	Country
Intelligence or Looks	Intelligence	Intelligence
Sprint or Stroll	Sprint	Stroll
Work or Play	Work	Work
Dreamer or Realist	Both	Both
Adventure or Romance	Romance	Adventure
Spontaneity or Routine	Spontaneity	Spontaneity
Today or Tomorrow	Today	Today
Debater or Mediator	Mediator	Mediator
Candlelight or Poker Night	Candlelight	Candlelight
Sunrise or Sunset	Sunrise	Sunrise
Cluttered or Organized	Organized	Cluttered
History or Art	History	Both
Land or Sea	Land	Both
Fiction or Nonfiction	Nonfiction	Nonfiction
Soup or Salad	Salad	Both

	Mel Klein	**Colleen Barrett**
Extrovert or Introvert	Extrovert	Extrovert
Love or Money	Love	Love
Old or New	Old	Old
Wisdom or Fame	Wisdom	Wisdom
Outside or Inside	Inside	Inside
Bungalow or Villa	Villa	Bungalow
SUV or Sports Car	Sports Car	Neither
Book or Movie	Both	Both
Hot & Spicy or Mild	Hot & Spicy	Mild
Town or Country	Both	Country
Intelligence or Looks	Both	Intelligence
Sprint or Stroll	Sprint	Sprint
Work or Play	Both	Both
Dreamer or Realist	Both	Realist
Adventure or Romance	Both	Romance
Spontaneity or Routine	Spontaneity	Routine
Today or Tomorrow	Today	Today
Debater or Mediator	Debater	Mediator
Candlelight or Poker Night	Both	Poker Night
Sunrise or Sunset	Sunset	Sunrise
Cluttered or Organized	Organized	Organized
History or Art	Both	Art
Land or Sea	Both	Sea
Fiction or Nonfiction	Nonfiction	Nonfiction
Soup or Salad	Both	Salad

—Acknowledgements—

I would like to take this chance to say thank you…

To my editor, Dan Moore, who happens to be my long-time friend and former college roommate. Dan, you are a virtuoso writer, and it was an honor for me to work with you.

To my publicist, Paul Mourraille, who is also a long-time friend, for his help in promoting this book. Paul, there is nothing like working with a fellow dreamer.

To my graphic designer, Scott Brown, for his genius and diligence. Scott, working with you has been an inspiration. I look forward to a growing friendship over the years.

To my other close friends including Mike Brown, Jay Goldstein, David Gutstadt, Shai Ingber, Damon Lee, Nickie Lum, Jeff Manderbaum, Scott Salinas, and Emil Zitser for their unconditional support over the years. Loyal friends are hard to come by. I particularly would like to thank Damon for his help on this book.

To my teachers in life, with special mention to my childhood athletic coach Brian McNamara and my trading mentor Ray Cahnman. Although life has moved on, I still think about you often. You have had a lasting impact on me.

To all the participants in this book, for believing in me, from the very beginning.

To all the people who have been so kind to me on my journey of writing this book; they include Susie Graves, Pete Kirsch, Laurie Weber, Ann Sweeney and the rest of the crew at

Greatbatch Enterprises, Emily Petterson, Grace Spivak, Ellen Yeske, Renee Boatman, Mary Wills, Liz Taylor, Eleanor Davis, Vickie Shuler, Jessica Kruvant-Wilson, Sharon Akers, Christine Amos and Patti Kelly.

To my wife's family for taking me in as one of their own. Mike, Cathy, Sean, Matt, Eddy, Rob, Gladys, and Laverne, you guys are the best.

To my parents, Joseph and Inna, my brother Matt, my sister Natasha, and my grandmother Tamara, for their unconditional love and support.

To my wife, who encouraged me every step of the way with her faith, strength and understanding. Tracy, you are my true love.

Whatever success this book realizes, it is a result of the people in my life.

Gene Katz